FOCUS ON

First Certificate

TEACHER'S BOOK

LONGMAN

SUE O'CONNELL

Addison Wesley Longman Limited
Edinburgh Gate, Harlow
Essex CM20 2JE England
and Associated Companies throughout the world

© Sue O'Connell 1996
First published by Harper Collins Publishers 1987

This edition first published by
Addison Wesley Longman Limited 1996

Set in Palatino

Printed in

ISBN 0 17 556998 3

Author acknowledgements

**The authors and publishers are grateful to the University of
Cambridge Local Examination Syndicate for their permission to
reproduce the information on page 8.**

▶ CONTENTS

	Introduction	6
UNIT 1	Taking a break	9
UNIT 2	Other people's jobs	11
UNIT 3	Enthusiasms	14
UNIT 4	Lawbreakers	17
UNIT 5	Waste not, want not	19
UNIT 6	The shape of things to come	22
UNIT 7	Going the hard way	25
UNIT 8	Family life	28
UNIT 9	Looking after yourself	31
UNIT 10	Narrow escapes	34
UNIT 11	The market place	37
UNIT 12	Turning points	39
	Exam Practice Use of English	43
	Exam Practice Listening	46
	Exam Practice Speaking	47
	Tapescripts	50

UNIT BY UNIT PLAN

	Reading texts	Grammar/Functions	Writing	Listening/Comm. activities	Study boxes/Exam practice
UNIT 1 Taking a break					
	1 I can't travel without... p.5 2 Dear travel agent... p.10	1 Review of present tenses p. 7 (Text 1) 2 Relative clauses p. 13 (Text 2) --- Likes and dislikes/preferences p. 4 Expressing need and use p. 16	1 Capital letters and punctuation p. 6 2 Describing a person p.19	1 Hotels p.12 2 Suitcases p. 18 CA 1 I can't travel without... p. 6 CA 2 Game p. 16	Phrasal verb catch p. 6 Phrasal verb live p. 15 Adjectives + prepositions p. 18 --- Language review p. 20
UNIT 2 Other people's jobs					
	1 Waiter for a week p.26 2 Work clothes p. 31	1 Adjectives and adverbs p. 24 2 The simple past p.28 3 The past continuous p.33 --- Disagreeing p.22	Informal letters p.36	1 Job opportunities p.23 2 A life at sea p. 35 CA Working can be a health hazard p.30	1 Expressions with do and make p. 30 2 The use of articles 1 p.36 3 Phrasal verb put p. 38 --- Language review p. 38
UNIT 3 Enthusiasms					
	1 Personal preferences p. 40 2 Keeping one jump ahead p. 49	1 The present perfect simple p. 43 (Text 1) 2 The present perfect continuous p.46 (Listening 1) 3 Modal verbs 2: ability p. 52	1 Paragraphing p. 45 2 Article p. 54	1 Hobbies p. 42 (Text 1) 2 The Bristol run p. 51 CA 20 questions p. 48	1 Adjective/Noun + Preposition: opposite p. 46 2 The order of adjectives p. 52 3 Adjectives with numbers p. 53 --- Language review p. 55
UNIT 4 Lawbreakers					
	1 Seven banks a day are robbed in LA p. 57 2 You're already well equipped to prevent crime p. 62 3 Granny, 70, holds up a bank! p. 66	1 Modal verbs 2: obligation p. 58 2 Participles p. 68 (Texts 1, 2, 3) --- Describing clothes p. 63	1 Report p. 60 2 Description p. 70	1 Crime report p. 61 2 Bad start to a honeymoon p. 65 CA Witness p. 63	1 steal vs. rob p. 56 2 Phrasal verb get (1) p. 61 3 Phrasal verb break p. 64 4 Compound adjectives p. 69 --- Language review p. 70
UNIT 5 Waste not, want not					
	1 A load of old rubbish? p. 73 2 Recycling p. 78 3 Friends of the Earth p. 80	1 Conditional 1 p. 74 2 Conditional 2 p. 81 3 Modal verbs 3: permission p. 86 --- Cause, result, addition, concession p. 83	Discussion p. 83	1 The sweet, short life of products p. 76 2 National parks p. 84 CA 1 Spot the difference (Pollution) p.77 CA 2 Follow the country code p. 82	1 Phrasal verb wear p 80 Prepositional phrases p. 80 2 Plural-form nouns p. 81 3 Phrasal verb set p. 85 --- Language review p. 88
UNIT 6 The shape of things to come					
	1 What's the big idea? p. 90 2 Super-watches p. 100	1 Talking about the future 1 p. 92 2 Sudden decisions, offers, suggestions, threats p. 95 3 Talking about the future 2 p. 97 --- Expressing sequence p. 95	1 Instructions p. 94 (Listening 1) 2 Description/Discussion p. 102 (Listening 2)	1 Word processor mishaps p. 93 2 Life in the future p. 96 CA 1 Role play– A new car phone p. 100 CA 2 Describe and draw p. 102	1 Phrasal verb let p. 96 2 Phrasal verb cut p. 103 --- Language review p. 103

	Reading texts	Grammar/Functions	Writing	Listening/Comm. activities	Study boxes/Exam practice
UNIT 7 Going the hard way					
	1 Freezing *p. 130* 2 Trisha Greenhalgh *p. 132* 3 The call of the wild *p. 138*	1 The gerund *p. 134* (Texts 1 and 2) 2 The past perfect *p. 139* (Texts 1, 2, 3) Describing objects *p. 144*	1 Formal letter 1 *p. 142* 2 Formal letter 2 *p. 144*	1 Overland to Australia *p. 132* 2 Polar explorer *p. 141* CA Quiz - How do you rate as a round-the-world rover? *p. 136*	1 The use of articles 2 *p. 129* 2 Phrasal verb *bring* *p. 136* 3 Verbs of perception *p. 141* Language review *p. 145* Odd man out *p. 146*
UNIT 8 Family life					
	1 Scruff justice *p. 148* 2 Working mothers: what children say *p. 154*	1 The infinitive *p. 150* (Text 1) 2 Reporting statements *p. 156* (Text 2) 3 Comparatives: *The...the...* *p. 160*	1 Part 1 Informal letter *p. 158* 2 Narrative *p. 161*	1 Children speaking *p. 153* 2 Single-parent family *p. 159* CA Spot the difference (beach scene) *p. 153*	1 Phrasal verb *look* *p. 152* 2 Phrasal verb *get* (2) *p. 158* 3 The use of articles 3 *p. 161* Language review *p. 162*
UNIT 9 Looking after yourself					
	1 Eating well *p. 164* 2 Cuts, bruises, bites, burns *p. 174*	1 Expressing quantity *p. 167* 2 Reported questions *p. 171* 3 Expressing number *p. 175* Describing food *p. 166*	1 Article *p. 169* 2 Report *p. 177*	1 Old wives' tales? *p. 166* 2 A first aid course *p. 173* CA Role play – The Laughing Cook Restaurant *p. 170*	1 Verb + preposition *p. 171* 2 Phrasal verb *come* *p. 177* Language review *p. 177* Odd man out *p. 178*
UNIT 10 Narrow escapes					
	1 Crew saves pilot *p. 180* 2 Rescue from the rapids *p. 186*	1 Expressing time *p.182* (Text 1) 2 Modal verbs 4: Certainty/probability/possibility *p. 188* 3 Question tags *p. 192* (Listening 2)	1 Instructions *p. 184* 2 Narrative *p. 194*	1 A survival kit *p. 184* 2 River drama *p. 190* CA 1 Puzzle *p. 187* CA 2 Brain-teasers *p. 191*	1 Purpose clauses *p. 188* 2 Prepositional phrases *p. 192* 3 Phrasal verb *go* *p. 193* Language review *p. 195*
UNIT 11 The market place					
	1 Down the aisle! *p. 197* 2 Buying by post *p. 200* 3 Advice for consumers *p. 205*	1 The passive voice *p. 198* (Text 1) 2 Gerund and infinitive *p. 206*	Part 1 Formal letter *p. 202*	1 Chips with everything *p. 200* 2 The auctioneer *p. 202* CA Selling pets *p. 204*	1 Have something done *p. 202* 2 Prepositional phrases *p. 203* Language review *p. 208*
UNIT 12 Turning points					
	1 Just a normal day? *p. 212* 2 Love in a strange climate *p. 218*	1 Expressing wishes and regrets *p. 210* 2 Conditional 3 *p. 217* 3 Review of tenses *p. 221* Contrast links, summing up *p. 223*	1 Exam practice – Formal letter *p. 214* Exam practice – Report *p. 215* 2 Exam practice – Informal letter *p. 223* Exam practice – Narrative *p. 223* Exam practice – Discussion *p. 223*	1 Is there life after redundancy? *p. 215* 2 A new direction *p. 222* CA Turning points in history *p. 216*	1 Phrasal verb *give* *p. 216* 2 Phrasal verb *take* *p. 220* Language review *p. 224*

Cross-references to related sections are given in brackets.

CA = Communications activity

INTRODUCTION

Focus on First Certificate is a complete, integrated course which practises all the skills needed to meet the requirements of the new syllabus of the *Cambridge First Certificate in English* examination. This new edition retains all the key features of the original highly successful course but it has been extensively revised to provide systematic preparation for all the new exam tasks. It also includes new exam practice sections for the Use of English, Listening and Speaking papers.

The material has been chosen to represent a wide range of contemporary written and spoken English. Reading material, which includes ten completely new texts, comes from newspapers, magazines, advertisements, and non-fiction writing of all kinds. The recordings include informal conversations, interviews with adults and children, monologues, and excerpts from various radio programmes. All the reading texts and a proportion of the listening texts are authentic, as in the examination itself.

The questions, exercises and activities based on this material include the full range of tasks for the revised examination – multiple choice, multiple matching, gapped text and so on – but they are not restricted to these alone. The aim has been to provide a balance between skills development work which is genuinely motivating and the necessary but narrower exam practice.

Focus on First Certificate also includes full grammar coverage, writing practice and a wide variety of communication activities. Special features are the **Study Boxes**, the **Exam Practice** material, the **Writing Bank** and the **Functions Bank**.

Vocabulary from the texts, the grammar sections and the Study Boxes is systematically revised in the Language Review sections of each unit.

▶ HOW TO USE THIS COURSE

Course organisation: The course is divided into twelve units, each with an 'umbrella' topic. There is a loose thematic link between units in the first half of the book and those in the second – for example, the holiday theme in Unit 1 links with that of travel in Unit 7 – and this allows for revision and recycling of topic vocabulary. In general, key skills are introduced and practised in Units 1–6, while in Units 7–12 there is a greater focus on exam tasks.

Timing: The time needed to work through a unit will vary according to the amount of class time spent on materials and activities and the amount set for homework. As a general rule, a unit is likely to take a minimum of six hours, and the whole course is likely to occupy 80–120 teaching hours.

Map of the book: There is a unit by unit plan on pages 4-5 of this book which shows the content of each unit of the Student's Book, with page references. In some cases there is a connection between two sections – a grammar presentation may be based on examples from an earlier

text, for example (as in Focus on grammar 1, Unit 1) or a writing task may arise from a communication activity (as in Unit 5). These connections are shown by references in brackets as a guide for those who plan to present sections in a different order from that of the book.

The Writing Bank: This is located in the centre of the book and provides models for each of the writing formats together with notes on layout and organisation, examples of useful language, and topics for further practice. It can be used for class study when a particular writing format is first introduced, and for reference and revision when students tackle similar writing tasks later. Page references to the Writing Bank are given throughout the book, and students should be encouraged to make full use of it as a valuable self-help resource.

The Functions Bank: This is also found in the centre of the book and can be used for the presentation of functional language or for the students to refer to before, during or after communication activities. By making frequent use of the Functions Bank in this way students will become more aware of the range of expressions available to them and can be encouraged to vary and extend their repertoire of language. Page references to the Functions Bank are given throughout the book.

Exam Practice sections: There are three Exam Practice sections towards the end of the book and these provide exam-format tasks for Papers 3 (Use of English), 4 (Listening) and 5 (Speaking). The tasks can be used individually at any stage of the course or they can be reserved for more intensive practice or 'mock' interviews as the exam approaches.

Index: There is a detailed index of structures and functions at the end of the book and it is useful to point this out to students so that they can make use of it to find the information they need on specific language items.

▶ A NOTE ON THE TEACHING APPROACH

The emphasis on communicative ability in the examination is reflected in the methodology underlying this course. Apart from the communication activities, there are many tasks where students are encouraged to collaborate by pooling their ideas or comparing their answers. Clearly this will only be useful if students use English to communicate!

If your students are not used to this method of working, and if they share a first language, it would be helpful to explain the purpose of the student-centred activities at the start of the course. Though they may find communicating in English frustrating at first, if they are willing to co-operate and persevere, they will notice a steady improvement in fluency and communicative ability. The long-term benefits will be well worth any initial difficulties.

▶ NOTES ON INDIVIDUAL SECTIONS

Lead-ins

These preliminary activities and discussions provide a very important jumping-off point for each unit. The aims are firstly to stimulate interest in a particular topic, secondly to involve students at a personal level and thirdly to revise and extend topic vocabulary.

Lead-in activities draw on whatever experience students already have of a topic and lead to an exchange of opinions and the pooling of information and language. By making a personal contribution in this way, students begin the unit with a sense of involvement and are more motivated to continue.

There is a wide variety of tasks, including quizzes and questionnaires, spotting deliberate mistakes and matching pictures to texts. Since they all require an element of student-centred work and the communication of personal choices or opinions to a partner or partners, they also practise skills and language needed for the Speaking paper in the examination.

Reading texts

There are 28 reading texts, of which 10 are completely new for this revised edition. They vary in length and style, reflecting a wide variety of authentic sources, including newspapers and magazines, advertisements and modern travel writing.

In most cases, texts have pre-questions to provide a reason for reading and to practise the skills of skimming and scanning which are essential both in the examination and for real-life reading tasks. It's important that students are trained to read quickly to answer these before they study a text more intensively.

There is a wide range of follow-up exercises with approximately one third being devoted to each of the exam reading tasks: multiple choice, multiple matching and gapped text. The vocabulary matching exercises and other vocabulary tasks are designed to develop the important skill of deducing the meaning of unknown words and so increase students' confidence in reading authentic material.

The exercises have been designed to highlight key language items. In general, it's not advisable to cover additional vocabulary in too much detail. Concentrating on unknown words can be discouraging and counter-productive in that it emphasises what students do *not* know, rather than what they do. This approach can also detract from overall understanding and spoil students' enjoyment of a reading task.

A selection of vocabulary from the texts in each unit is revised in the Language Review sections. These vocabulary items are listed in the Teacher's Notes for each text so that the teacher can draw them to the students' attention if necessary.

Focus on grammar

Each unit has either two or three grammar sections and these cover all the main areas tested in the *First Certificate* examination. It is assumed that most students will already have met most of this grammar during the course of their studies and so the grammar sections here are designed to review and summarise the key points, and to provide practice and revision exercises.

More extensive grammar and vocabulary practice is provided in *Focus on First Certificate Grammar Practice* (Richard Walton) in the same series.

Study boxes

There are between two and four Study Boxes in each unit, usually relating to language which is used in the reading or listening texts. These isolate a number of language items which are frequently tested in the examination and which students should make a special point of learning. Areas covered include dependent prepositions and prepositional phrases, phrasal verbs, compound adjectives and the order of adjectives.

Items from the Study Boxes are tested in the Language Review sections. They are also practised in *Focus on First Certificate Grammar Practice* (Richard Walton).

Focus on listening

There are two listening texts in each unit and these are recorded on two accompanying cassettes, which remain the same for this revised edition. The tapescripts are reproduced at the end of this book.

The recordings include a mixture of scripted and authentic material, as in the examination itself, and represent both formal and informal contexts.

There is a wide variety of question-types designed to develop students' listening skills and these include multiple choice, true/false, and blank-filling. Always allow time for students to read through the instructions and question(s), and check that they understand these. Each recording should be played through twice. When checking answers to the questions, useful language points can be highlighted. Any vocabulary items included in the Language Review are listed in the Teacher's Notes.

Note: The Exam Practice section at the end of the book has eight additional listening tasks in the format of the revised examination.

Focus on writing

These sections cover all the kinds of writing required in Paper 2 of the examination. They are supplemented by reference material and further practice tasks in the Writing Bank.

Each of the main writing tasks (letters, articles, reports and various types of composition) is introduced along with its key features. These are recycled in later units and Unit 12 includes all the task-types as a final revision.

Throughout the course, there is an emphasis on the importance of planning written work, and many writing sections include activities in which students prepare in groups prior to the writing stage.

Communication activities

The aim of these activities is to provide an opportunity for the freer, more creative use of language, with the emphasis on *communication* rather than accuracy. In this way they also develop the oral skills needed for the Speaking paper of the examination. Activities include games and role plays, quizzes, brain teasers, 'spot the difference' and 'describe and draw' activities. Overall there is a balance between activities where students compete to achieve a goal and activities where they co-operate.

Many activities include references to the Functions Bank and this can be used by students before an activity for initial practice or referred to briefly during an activity.

Discourage students from leaving their books open at the Functions Bank or referring to it too much, however, since communication will inevitably be less fluent as a result. Another way of using the Functions Bank is for students to refer to it *after* an activity so that they can make a note of expressions which they have not used and bear them in mind for the future.

The Teacher's Notes give guidance in preparing students for the activities and following up afterwards. In general, once the necessary preparation has taken place, students should be able to carry on with a minimum of assistance from the teacher. On-the-spot correction, however tempting, is to be avoided though notes of major or recurring mistakes can be made to be dealt with at a later stage.

Language reviews

These sections consist of multiple choice questions revising language from the unit. The correct answers come from one of the reading or listening texts, from a Study Box or from a grammar section. Units 6 and 12 also revise items from previous units. References to the sources of these items are given in the Teacher's Notes so that students can be reminded of their original contexts.

▶ In addition, two units have 'odd man out' exercises which serve to review an area of topic vocabulary.

Exam practice sections

These three sections provide exam-format tasks which can be used at any stage of the course or reserved for more intensive exam preparation towards the end of the course.

Use of English Five complete papers each including five tasks: multiple choice and open cloze, 'key' word transformations, error correction and word formation.

Listening Eight listening tasks practising all the task types which can appear in the Listening paper: multiple choice, note taking, blank filling, multiple matching, selection from two or three possible answers.

Speaking Five papers practising the two central parts of the Speaking paper: talking about photographs and taking part in a communication task.

An outline of the revised examination

The revised FCE retains the format of five papers. Each paper is equally weighted

Paper	Name	Timing	Contents	Test Focus
Paper 1	Reading	1 hour 15 minutes	4 long texts, or 3 long and 2 or more short texts; 35 reading comprehension questions.	Assessment of candidates' ability to: understand gist, main points, detail, text structure or specific information, or deduce meaning in written texts.
Paper 2	Writing	1 hour 30 minutes	1 compulsory task; 4 tasks from which candidates select 1.	Assessment of candidates' ability to: write specific text types for a specified audience and purpose; letters, articles, reports or composition.
Paper 3	Use of English	1 hour 15 minutes	5 tasks (65 questions) focusing on grammar and vocabulary.	Assessment of candidates' ability to: demonstrate knowledge of lexical and grammatical systems.
Paper 4	Listening	40 minutes (approx)	2 longer recorded texts and 2 series of shorter extracts; 30 listening comprehension questions.	Assessment of candidates' ability to: understand gist, main points, detail or specific information, or deduce meaning in spoken texts.
Paper 5	Speaking	15 minutes (approx)	A 4-phase interaction between 2 candidates and an interlocutor/assessor. For assessment purposes a second assessor will also be present.	Assessment of candidates' ability to: exchange personal and factual information; express and find out about attitudes and opinions.

UNIT NOTES AND KEY

UNIT 1 ▶ Taking a break

▶ Lead-in (p. 4)

Before students open their books, introduce the topic orally. For example, ask students to work in pairs to find out about each other's last holiday. Then each student should report back briefly on what their partner has told them.

First ask students to identify the types of holiday shown in the pictures: **A** camping; **B** beach/seaside; **C** cruise; **D** safari; **E** mountain walking/hiking; **F** skiing.

You could also introduce some topic vocabulary at this stage, but it's best to keep the introduction fairly brief.

1 As students do the first task, emphasise that money is no object!

2 While students work in pairs on the second task, it's useful to monitor and note particular errors and language needs.

3 Instead of referring students to the Functions Bank, you may prefer to present the relevant language on the board and practise it orally.

Vocabulary included in the Language review: can't bear, keen on (Functions Bank).

▶ Text 1 I can't travel without ... (p. 5)

As an introduction, ask students to describe the picture and discuss what kind of person it represents.

1 C *(travelling light)*
2 B *(keep a diary)*
3 E *(penknife ... I have never used it)*
4 A *(correspondence)*
5 B *(sketch book)*, also possibly C *(notebooks)*
6 D *(credit card)*
7 B *(new diary)*

Note: Students who finish quickly can check their answers together.

Vocabulary included in the Language review: do without (line 1), catch up with (A, line 2 ; see also Study Box 1), fill with, (B, line 1), except (B, line 5), at a moment's notice, (D, line 4).

▶ Communication activity 1 (p. 6)

The clearest way to set up this activity is to give students the name of a suitable object (such as an alarm clock) and then ask them questions until you 'guess' the answer. You may want to practise some question forms first if necessary.

Make sure everyone has chosen an object before pairwork begins. Again, students can report back on their partner's chosen object at the end.

▶ Focus on writing 1 Capital letters and punctuation

Capital letters
1

1	e.g. Patrick Lichfield	5	Italy
2	Virgin Atlantic Airways	6	Milan
3	Olympus Pearlcorder	7	Swiss
4	Daily Mail	8	TV

2
1 Mona Lisa, The Merchant of Venice
2 the Middle East, South Australia
3 Wall Street, Trafalgar Square
4 the Amazon, the Pacific Ocean
5 Jupiter, Mars
6 Christmas, the Middle Ages
7 Doctor White, Professor Smith

Punctuation
1

1	full stop	4	exclamation mark
2	comma	5	apostrophe
3	question mark	6	quotation marks (inverted commas)

2
1 b
2 e
3 d
4 f
5 a
6 c

3 Exercise
a I haven't told you where we're going this summer, have I? Well, we've decided to go to Nepal in July.
b Ken read an article about it in a Sunday newspaper, you see, and he was so enthusiastic that I said, 'Why don't we go?'
c We'll be flying to Kathmandu and then touring the east of the country.
d It'll be a chance to see Mount Everest although we certainly won't be climbing it!
e By the way, I'm going to a lecture at the library next Friday. Professor Sweeting will be talking about his recent trip to the Himalayas. Would you like to come too?

▶ Focus on grammar 1 Review of the present tenses (p. 7)

Exercise 1
a The kettle is boiling; Water boils
b I'm living; I live
c He plays; He's playing
d it's raining; it rains
e We usually bath; the children are bathing

The present simple
The following are examples:
1 a wins
  b falls
2 stops

The present continuous
1 a The telephone's ringing
  b I'm working
2 we're ... going/travelling

Exercise 2

a	I'm looking	f	I see
b	he has	g	you think
c	He's thinking	h	are you seeing
d	This jug holds	i	My parents are having
e	You look	j	Who's holding

Exercise 3
a What are you doing; We're spending
b Oil and water do not mix; Oil floats
c Why are you cooking; You know; Helen only eats
d I don't understand; he's saying; Is he speaking

e   I normally go; I'm working
f   I know; you mean; I don't agree
g   I do; he cooks; we both give

Text 2 (p. 10)

1 You may find this opening stage works better if you write the headline on the board and ask students to discuss it with their books closed.

2 Give students just enough time to read the first paragraph. Don't let them read on yet.

3 This is a gentle introduction to one of the new reading tasks in the First Certificate exam, the 'gapped text'. Tell students to read the text through fairly quickly first, without worrying about the gaps. Then encourage them to read the four quotations and to look for clues about where they should come in the text. Ask, for example, what A could follow (a question); what B could describe (a house/car/holiday); and who 'they' might be in C.

| 1 | D | 3 | A |
| 2 | B | 4 | C |

4

1 False ('*petty, silly little things*')
2 True ('*fails to live up to the brochure promises*')
3 True ('*baby minding*')
4 True ('*an initial complaint*')
5 False ('*eventually*')
6 True ('*self-catering*')
7 True ('*do their research*')
8 False (*only from those who have complained and are 'unhappy with the response'*)

5

1	deluge	6	issued a summons
2	petty	7	met in full
3	package	8	furious
4	cots	9	hurricane
5	practically non-existent	10	conciliation facilities

8

1	by	5	On
2	in	6	up
3	of	7	with
4	as; for	8	to; about

Vocabulary included in the Language review: complain about (line 7), fail to (line 10), attracted by (line 13), described as (line 14), do research (line 41), free of charge (line 51).

Focus on listening 1 (p. 12)

| 1 The Atlantic | 2 The Plaza |
| 3 The Concord | 4 The Royal |

5 Days: Fridays and Tuesdays
6 Time: Third week in July
7 Price: From £159 to £191
8 Insurance: The most expensive: £14.25
                          The cheapest: £10.80

Check/recap by asking students to describe the buildings orally. (They could also do this in writing as consolidation.)

Useful vocabulary: look through, pick out, end up; three-storey building, terrace, the rear; curved, situated, steps (versus stairs); to screen ... from; a (steep) slope, balconies, break up (of schools).

Focus on grammar 2 Relative clauses (p.13)

Exercise 1

| a | defining | c | non-defining |
| b | non-defining | d | defining |

Exercise 2

1	f who/that	6	i which/that
2	e which/that	7	j that
3	g that	8	c which/that
4	a who/that	9	h whose
5	d whose	10	b which/that

The relative pronoun can be omitted from sentences 3, 6, 7, 8, and 10.

Exercise 3

a   The house (*that*) we used to live in has just been sold.
b   The old lady *who* lives across the road has got eight cats.
c   The friend (*who/that*) you were looking for has just come in.
d   The old chair (*which/that*) my grandmother left me in her will is worth a fortune.
e   I bought my watch at a local shop *whose* name I can't remember.
f   The writer *whose* latest book was published on Tuesday lives in New York.
g   The neighbour *who* has been to Sao Paulo says he's never seen anything like it.
h   The blouse (*which/that*) I gave Helen for her birthday is worn out already.
i   The student *who* came top in maths at school has gone to university.
j   None of the people (*who/that*) went to Paris this spring complained about the hotel.

Exercise 4 (Example answers)

a ... *which* (is famous for its tennis tournament)
b ... *which* (are to be held in ...)
c ... *whose* (name is ...)
d ... *who* (reached the New World in 1492.)
e ... *which* (is in the Himalayas)

Exercise 5

Commas are needed in sentences b, d and g. The relative pronoun can be omitted in sentences c and f.

Communication activity 2 (p. 16)

1 Vocabulary and definitions

You may prefer your students to keep their books closed while you cover this preparatory section. In this case, choose suitable examples of objects (such as *pen, microscope, saw, key, clothes*) and elicit from students the various ways of defining them.

The practice activities in 3 and 4 can both be done in pairs or groups.

2 Game

Preparation

Equipment: It will save time if you are able to prepare the three sets of paper for each group in advance. If this is not possible, ask each group to read the instructions and to prepare their own slips beforehand. Check that these are correct before proceeding.

Note: It is helpful if the numbers and letters are written on different colours of paper (or in a different colour ink) so that they can be easily distinguished.

Language: Again, you may prefer to present a selection of useful language on the board and practise it, rather than refer students to the Functions Bank at this stage.

Procedure

Ideally, students should be grouped in small circles round tables. Even if desks are fixed, however, it is usually possible to move chairs so that this arrangement is achieved.

Tell students to pick a slip in order to decide which holiday they're going on. Ask them to decide specific details: where it is, when it is, and for how long.

Ask them to read through the instructions, and check that these are understood.

Once the game has started, make sure each group is playing according to the rules and scoring correctly.

Encourage players to ask questions and to challenge each other.

Discourage too much argument! Some students may feel they mustn't allow any points, however justified!

Note any language errors and gaps for attention later.

Feedback

Ask groups to report back on the results of their games. Deal with any important language problems.

▶ Focus on listening 2 (p.18)

1 Vocabulary check

lock, label, handle, catch, buckle, zip, strap, padlock

2   1 expensive and heavy

2 toughness (strength)

3 to get damaged

4

	Riviera	Windsor	Tornado	Mayfair
a Length	67 cm	68 cm	75 cm	80 cm
b Material	PVC	nylon	ABS	aluminium
c Fastening/Security	zip+padlock	catches	2 locks	2 locks
d Number of wheels	4	2	2	2
e Strap or Handle for pushing/pulling	strap	strap	handle	handle
f Price	£67	£32.50	£109.50	£199
d Tester's verdict	good value for money	good value but material might get torn	strong but heavy	smart and practical but over priced

Vocabulary included in the Language review: label

▶ Focus on writing 2 Description (p. 19)

1   Make sure that students are clear about what they have to do before they begin. Monitor the discussions to help with ideas and to encourage self-correction if there are any mistakes. Try to check that all the questions are correct before continuing.

2   Monitor the interviews and encourage students to ask additional questions, if necessary, to find out more detailed or interesting information. Keep a note of mistakes and feed back to students on any important points before the next stage.

3   This can be done as group or class discussion. The former will probably be more productive but the latter can be done more quickly if time is short.

▶ Language review (p. 20)

1	D (Text 1, B)	9	A (Lead-in, Study Box 3)
2	B (Text 1, B)	10	C (Text 2)
3	C (Text 2)	11	C (Text 1, A; Study Box 1)
4	A (Text 1, D)	12	A (Text 2)
5	D (Text 2)	13	B (Text 2)
6	C (Listening 2)	14	D (Text 1)
7	D (Study Box 2)	15	B (Text 2)
8	B (Functions Bank)		

UNIT 2 ▶ Other people's jobs

▶ Lead-in 1 (p. 21)

Ask students to work together to identify the ten jobs as quickly as possible (5 minutes) and check their answers. Check relevant vocabulary for equipment too at this stage.

1 florist (bouquet); **2** plumber (tap,spanner); **3** firefighter (helmet, hose); **4** window cleaner (bucket, ladder, sponge); **5** painter (paintbrush, tin of paint); **6** dustman (dustbin); **7** hairdresser (scissors, comb, hairdryer); **8** architect/draughtsman (drawing board); **9** lorry driver (cab); **10** dentist (dentist's surgery, chair)

Allow students a few moments to think about the questions before they discuss the answers in pairs or small groups. Tell them they **must** finally agree on one job for each category and be prepared to give reasons for their choice.

Monitor the discussions and notice any errors and language needs, particularly in the area of comparatives and superlatives (Focus on grammar 1).

▶ Lead-in 2 (p. 21)

1   Check that students understand the introduction and what they have to do. Don't refer them to the table on page 22 at this stage.

After sufficient reading and discussion time, invite possible answers and ask students to say which words or phrases helped them to guess the jobs. Don't confirm or deny any of the suggestions yet.

2   Refer students to the table on page 22 and, when this has been considered, confirm final answers.

Place	Extract	Job
Photographic Studio	C	Male model
Museum	B	Museum attendant
Restaurant	D	Waiter
Holiday Resort	A	Holiday representative

3   Ask students to compare their answers when they have finished this exercise. Again, ask them to justify their answers by saying which words or phrases helped them.

1   D (apron, valet's jacket), also possibly B
2   D (the place is jumping, etc.)
3   C (agony of indecision, embarrassment)
4   A (broken tap, lost wallet), B
5   B (I saw my life ticking by)
6   D (the thrill of a film star)
7   A (Alan)

4 Discussion points

b   Ask students to report back briefly on their discussions.

5 Disagreeing

Practise the language in the table and examples orally, with attention to stress and intonation, before students start pair work.

6   This can be an optional writing exercise. Ask students to answer the questions in 150–200 words.

Vocabulary included in the Language review: a while (extract A), during (extract C), interest in (extract C).

▶ Focus on listening 1 (p. 23)

1   a Cost: free.
    b Young Engineer of the Year Competition: closing date: end of May; prize: £1,000.

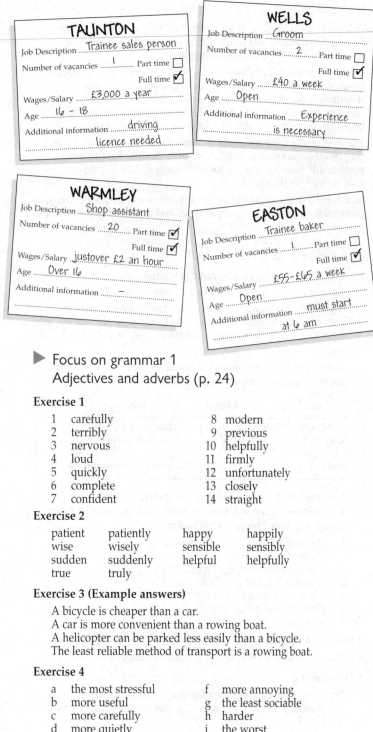

TAUNTON
Job Description ..... Trainee sales person
Number of vacancies ..... 1 ..... Part time ☐
Full time ☑
Wages/Salary ..... £3,000 a year
Age ..... 16 – 18
Additional information ..... driving
licence needed

WELLS
Job Description ..... Groom
Number of vacancies ..... 2 ..... Part time ☐
Full time ☑
Wages/Salary ..... £40 a week
Age ..... Open
Additional information ..... Experience
is necessary

WARMLEY
Job Description ..... Shop assistant
Number of vacancies ..... 20 ..... Part time ☑
Full time ☑
Wages/Salary ..... just over £2 an hour
Age ..... Over 16
Additional information ..... –

EASTON
Job Description ..... Trainee baker
Number of vacancies ..... 1 ..... Part time ☐
Full time ☑
Wages/Salary ..... £55–£65 a week
Age ..... Open
Additional information ..... must start
at 6 am

▶ Focus on grammar 1
Adjectives and adverbs (p. 24)

Exercise 1

1 carefully
2 terribly
3 nervous
4 loud
5 quickly
6 complete
7 confident
8 modern
9 previous
10 helpfully
11 firmly
12 unfortunately
13 closely
14 straight

Exercise 2

patient   patiently   happy   happily
wise   wisely   sensible sensibly
sudden   suddenly   helpful   helpfully
true   truly

Exercise 3 (Example answers)

A bicycle is cheaper than a car.
A car is more convenient than a rowing boat.
A helicopter can be parked less easily than a bicycle.
The least reliable method of transport is a rowing boat.

Exercise 4

a the most stressful
b more useful
c more carefully
d more quietly
e fitter
f more annoying
g the least sociable
h harder
i the worst
j the most expensive

▶ Text 1 Waiter for a week (p. 26)

You could introduce the topic by asking students, either in pairs or as a class, to say what the best/worst things about being a waiter would be.

This is a simple example of the 'gapped text' question in the exam. Explain that the best approach is to read through the text quickly first, ignoring the gaps. You could ask one or two questions to check

general understanding at this stage.

Then encourage students to look for clues in the sentences which will help them to place them correctly. Perhaps the easiest ones to start with are E and A. Point out different articles in *the commis* (C) and *a commis* (D) and ask which is likely to come first.

1

1 D   4 A
2 E   5 B
3 C

2

1 Fetching orders, helping to serve, clearing tables, etc.
2 The long hours.
3 The distance of the restaurant from the kitchen.
4 The way they called him or ignored him.

3 Vocabulary

1 B   5 B
2 A   6 C
3 C   7 C
4 A

4 True/false

1 False (It's the senior waiter's responsibility.)
2 False (They share the tips equally.)
3 True (*What can you do ...?*)
4 False (*The commis then comes up ...*)
5 True (*yelling, banging, hissing*)
6 True (*You need ... to stay out of trouble.*)
7 False (*Deference, a quality I usually lack.*)
8 True

5 Discussion points

For variety, section A points can be discussed by the class as a whole and section B by the students in small groups.

Vocabulary included in the Language review: work as a team (line 2), although (line 8), responsible for (line 13), wrist (line 54), treat (67).

▶ Focus on grammar 2 The simple past (p. 28)

Exercise 1

a in   f when
b during   g until
c ago   h after
d at   i before
e for   j on

Exercise 2 (Example answers)

a ... hated taking examinations.
b ... sent him to bed.
c ... rarely travelled abroad.
d ... I played a lot of tennis.
e ... did you like best?

Form 1 Regular verbs

dance   danced   stop   stopped
argue   argued   tap   tapped
use   used   rot   rotted
prefer   preferred   try   tried
occur   occurred   apply   applied
travel   travelled   study   studied

Form 2 Irregular verbs

Infinitive	Past	Past Participle
become	became	become
bite	bit	bitten
break	broke	broken
catch	caught	caught
choose	chose	chosen
cost	cost	cost
drive	drove	driven

fall	fell	fallen
feel	felt	felt
fly	flew	flown
hear	heard	heard
lay	laid	laid
lose	lost	lost
put	put	put
ride	rode	ridden
shoot	shot	shot
steal	stole	stolen
teach	taught	taught
tear	tore	torn
write	wrote	written

▶ **Communication activity Working can be a health hazard (p. 30)**

Introduction

You may prefer to introduce the subject of stress orally, rather than by reading through the text on page 30. The main points to be covered in a discussion are:

What is stress? What causes it? (danger, pressure of work, frustration)

What jobs have high stress? Which have low stress? (avoiding examples on the list, if possible)

What are the results of stress? How can we overcome stress?

The task

Check that students understand the instructions and that they know all the jobs on the list. Ask one student in each pair to be responsible for drawing up the three groups of jobs on a separate piece of paper. Emphasise that they must agree on their groups and be prepared to say **why** they have put particular jobs in particular groups.

Set a time limit of 10 minutes for the activity, and monitor progress.

As pairs finish, ask them to compare their results briefly with those of other pairs. Check that they have remembered to select a job with the highest stress and one with the lowest.

Feedback

Check first on students' choices of highest-stress and lowest-stress jobs, asking them to give reasons. Allow other students to disagree or challenge.

Then ask each pair to suggest one other high-stress job on their list, and one low-stress job, giving reasons. Discuss briefly.

Finally refer students to the official results on page 228 of their book, and again discuss possible reasons for the high or low ranking of particular jobs — especially those which differ from the students' ranking.

Optional additional activity

This can be used to start or finish a lesson. Ask students in pairs to write down three people who:

— work with animals
— travel for their work
— work with their hands
— sometimes risk their lives in their work

▶ **Text 2 (p. 31)**

1 If students don't know *bouncer* or *barrister*, see if the pictures help them to guess. Allow time to revise basic clothes vocabulary from the pictures and to discuss their reactions to the different styles.

2 Check that students understand the four headings in each section before they begin reading. This is an example of the 'multiple matching' type of question in the examination.

Discourage slow detailed reading and encourage scanning by setting a time limit (2–3 minutes).

1 The bouncer
2 The school pupil
3 The bouncer
4 The barrister

For questions 3 and 4, allow time for detailed reading and ask students to compare answers in pairs as they finish. When checking, make sure they can justify their answers.

3

1	B	5	D
2	D	6	B
3	A	7	C
4	C	8	A

4

1 C
2 B
3 D
4 B

Vocabulary included in the Language review: spend (money) on (Question 2), strict (B), advise (C), to tap (someone) (C).

▶ **Focus on grammar 3 The past continuous (p. 33)**

Exercise 1 (Example answers)

a ... was enjoying herself on holiday.
b ... was having a bath.
c ... sold the house.
d ... broke in.
e ... was already working.
f ... had to walk or ride.
g ... pulled into the space.
h ... had a party to celebrate.
i ... were sunbathing in the garden.
j ... was waiting outside another.

Exercise 2

1	happened	11	was heading
2	was working	12	began
3	usually cycled	13	moved
4	was trying	14	went
5	was just beginning	15	came
6	left	16	was lying
7	thought	17	were standing
8	got	18	heard
9	cycled	19	sank
10	turned	20	arrived

▶ **Focus on listening 2 A life at sea (p.35)**

Introduction

Explain that students are going to hear an interview with a man who worked as a merchant seaman (explain what the merchant navy is, if necessary).

Ask students to read through the six statements in the first part, and the four multiple choice questions in the second part. Check that there are no vocabulary problems in the question. (Note: tell them that 'bellboy' will be explained during the recording.)

True/false

1 False. (*it was an idea I went along with*)
2 False. (*he wasn't needed*)
3 True. (*how to lay a table ... carry cups and saucers and plates ...*)
4 True. (difficult conditions, strict discipline)
5 False. (he had to stand by the bellboard and wait for the bells to ring)
6 False. (he never questioned what he was doing)

Multiple choice

7 D (six years plus four years)
8 B (the living quarters were very poor — iron bunks, no carpets, etc.)
9 D (the ship would have been smashed against the quay)
10 C (he was finally convinced by people that it was time to leave)

▶ Focus on writing Informal letters (p. 36)

1/2 Check that students' completed versions of the two tasks on page 36 are correct, since these can be used as models for the writing task which follows.

Check comprehension of the letter by asking, for example, why the writer is writing to Gill, and what changes there have been in his/her life.

3 1 False: Never write your name before your address.
2 True
3 False: Never begin 'Dear Friend'; always use a name.
4 False: Write the first line next to the margin.
5 True
6 True
7 False: Write the end of the letter near the middle of the page.
8 True

Note: It would be useful to have a brief revision of these points in a later lesson.

4 5 paragraphs: Introduction/Beginning; First piece of news; Second piece of news; Invitation; Ending

5 If there is time, get students to begin working on ideas for their letters in class. This way you can encourage them to get into the habit of making a plan for writing tasks, and you can also check ideas and language beforehand.

▶ Language review (p. 38)

1	D (2C)	9	B (1.13)
2	D (Lead-in 2C)	10	B (1.2)
3	C (Lead-in 2A)	11	D (Lead-in 2C)
4	B (2C)	12	A (1.67)
5	C (2B)	13	C (2)
6	C (Focus on grammar 3)	14	B (1.54)
7	A (Study Box 3)	15	D (1.8)
8	A (Study Box 2)		

▶ Lead-in (p. 40)

You could introduce this activity by drawing two or three pieces of equipment connected with **your** hobby and asking students to guess what it is. This could lead to a brief class discussion about hobbies in general.

Tell students they don't need to put down the exact word for an item – a general word will do (for example, paints for artist's palette). Give them a few minutes to work on their own, and then ask them to compare their answers with a neighbour's and try to complete the rest.

Activity	Sewing	Gardening	Painting	Tennis	Cooking
Item 1	sewing machine	spade	(picture) frame	racket	saucepan
Item 2	cotton/thread	(pot) plant	paints/palette	net	scales
Item 3	scissors	(wellington) boots	paint brush	ball	knife
Item 4	needle	watering can	canvas/easel	tennis shoes	whisk

▶ Text 1 (p.40)

1 See whether any students can explain *windsurfing* and *budgerigar breeding* before they look at the key in the book. Ask them to read the descriptions of the four people and the clues to their hobbies. Check or teach *aggressive* and *aggressiveness*.

Ask students to guess what the four hobbies could be before they read the texts.

2 A Rosalind Plowright; B Geoff Capes; C Bill Sirs; D Sally Oppenheim.

Ask students to explain how they decided on their answers.

3 A *You can really get away from it all, a tremendous escape.*
B *The hobby gives me relaxation and peace of mind.*
C *It releases the tensions of work.*
D *When you're playing it, you can't think of anything else.*

All four find their hobby a way of relaxing and escaping from the pressures of their work.

4 Multiple choice

1	A	2	C
3	C		
4	B		
5	A	6	C
7	D		
8	A	9	D
10	B		
11	A	12	C
13	B	14	D

5 1 exhilarating
2 claustrophobia
3 tensions
4 aggressiveness
5 frustration
6 elation

Vocabulary included in the Language review: A: tend to (be), conscious of, keep fit; B: the opposite of, compete in; C: apart from + ing, approve of, in that case; D: *for* fun, score.

▶ Focus on listening 1 (p. 42)

Revise *windsurfing, budgerigar breeding* and check *judo*.

Give students time to read through the tasks and answer any questions.

Activity	First Introduced	Made an Olympic Event	Costs	
Judo	1882	1964	Judo suit to buy	£ 15
			Judo suit to hire	£5 a month
Windsurfing	1969	1984	Beginners board	£ 300
			A racing board	£ 1,000
Budgerigar Breeding	1840	X	Price range for birds	£ 7 –£500

1 headquarters
2 March – September
3 dry suit
4 01-127 3444
5 pink

▶ Focus on grammar 1
The present perfect simple (p. 43)

Exercise 1

a since
b for
c for
d since
e since

Exercise 2

a He's lost a lot of hair.
b He's grown a moustache.
c His eyesight has got worse.
d He's put on weight.
e He's changed his style of dress.

Exercise 3

a Have you ever been to the opera?
b Have they arrived yet?
c She has never learned to drive.
d I still haven't finished that book.
e Your father hasn't phoned yet.

Exercise 4

1 i
2 h
3 j
4 g
5 b
6 d
7 f
8 a
9 c
10 e

▶ Focus on writing 1 Paragraphing (p. 45)

1

1 The three paragraphs should begin:
The world's oldest ski ...
There are two main forms of skiing: ...
The world's best skiers compete each winter ...
2 C, E, A

2

1D, 2B, 3A, 4C

2 B: The long hours of practice; A: The hard work; C: Why people enjoy ice hockey.
3 2: The long hours ('Some go on until 3 am.') + 3: 'And if the *hours* weren't bad enough';
3: The hard work ('the training sessions are very *hard work*') + 4: 'so much *effort*'

3 1 b, 2 d, 3 a, 4 e, 5 c. (It would also be possible to put c first in order to warn the reader in advance and get their attention.)

4 Example answers

1 a Advantages of camping; b Buying equipment; c Choosing a camp site; d Dos and don'ts
2 a Deciding on the place; b Designing invitations; c Providing food; d Organising party games; e Letting people know it's time to go home

▶ Focus on grammar 2
The present perfect continuous (p. 46)

Exercise 1 (Example answers)

a Because she's been crying.
b Because I've been running.
c Because he's been digging in the garden.
d Because I've been doing a lot of overtime.

Exercise 2

a I've been sharing; came
b left; applied; has been working
c saw; have never read
d have you been standing
e have been; rejected
f Have you heard; have announced; have been going out; thought
g have you been doing; have seen; met
h have been; have warned; have already occurred
i haven't heard; wrote
j have risen; joined

▶ Communication activity 20 questions (p. 48)

Read through the instructions with the class and make sure they are understood.

Expand the list of possible questions, as suggested in the book, imagining that the activity in question is football.

Acting as Subject yourself, start the activity off. Choose a fairly easy hobby which students are likely to be able to guess without too much difficulty.

With a class which is larger than 16, it's probably best to divide students into two or more groups. Try to include a range of ability in each group.

Monitor the activity, but avoid interrupting if possible. Make it clear that everyone must listen out for mistakes in the questions, and that the Subject can only answer correct questions.

▶ Text 2 Keeping one jump ahead (p. 49)

You could introduce the topic by asking students to name as many dangerous sports as they can (and mention any they do themselves, of course) and discussing what makes people take up activities like these.

1 1 He jumps off tall buildings wearing a parachute.
2 When he doesn't have permission to jump he may be arrested and fined.

2 a warm to you
b bear in mind
c busted
d mishap
e took a flying leap
f loony
g wimp
h objected to

3 1 C
2 B
3 D
4 A
5 C
6 B

Vocabulary included in the Language review: beat (a record) (line 7), bear in mind (line 28), at the latest (line 30), object to (line 35).

▶ Focus on listening 2 (p. 51)

Introduction

Discuss the difference between jogging and running (briefly) and the benefits (and possible dangers) of long-distance running.

Ask students to look carefully at the map of Bristol on page 51 and to locate:

the **City Centre**
Neptune's Statue
the **Hotel**
the **SS Great Britain**
Clifton Village
the **Suspension Bridge**

1 Ask them to read through the four multiple choice questions (1–4).

Note: The listening text provides a number of examples of the language of describing directions, for example: *I turned sharp left; I took the first turning on the left.*

The most useful way of checking the map is to ask students to describe exactly what directions the runner took.

2 Multiple choice

1 B (He doesn't *carry any money on him*; the 2p fee prevented him from crossing.)
2 B (It had a production of 'The Sound of Music'.)
3 A (He set out to run 5 miles and did so.)
4 C (*even if it is hilly*).

Additional activities

Here are some suggestions for further practice in giving and following directions:

1 Students study the Functions Bank on page 108.

2 Using the map of Bristol, students work in pairs. Student A decides on a starting point and destination, and a route between them. S/he gives Student B the starting point and then gives directions without mentioning the destination. Student B follows the directions and sees where s/he ends up!

Note: It is best if A cannot see B's map for this activity.

3 Using a different map, students again work in pairs and reverse roles for the same activity.

▶ Focus on grammar 3 Modal verbs 1: ability (p. 52)

Exercise 1

a	could; can	f	haven't been able to
b	will never be able to	g	was able to
c	could; was able to	h	couldn't
d	could have	i	I'll be able to
e	Can	j	was able to

▶ Focus on writing 2 Article (p. 54)

Preparation

Go through all the planning stages in class. This will help students get used to analysing the question and asking the all-important questions: What *kind* of writing do I have to do? *Who* am I writing to? What is the *purpose*?

Encourage students to think carefully about their readers and to use their imagination to find ways of making their article interesting and readable.

Check each student's plan as a way of forestalling mistakes and emphasising the importance of the planning stage. Remind them to look through the section on articles in the Writing Bank.

1
1 an article
2 students
3 to describe an activity and encourage others to take it up
4 100–150 words

2 Example answers
1 18–21
2 Fairly informal
3 Design an interesting headline; make the first sentence interesting/unusual/surprising – a question can be a good starting point.
4 Include some humour; don't put in too much detail; emphasise all the positive points about the activity.

▶ Language review (p. 55)

1	C (1D)	6	B (2.28)	11	A (1C)
2	A (1A)	7	D (1C)	12	D (2.7)
3	D (1A)	8	C (1B)	13	A (2.29)
4	A (1D)	9	C (1B)	14	D (2.35)
5	B (1C)	10	B (1C)	15	D (Study Box 1)

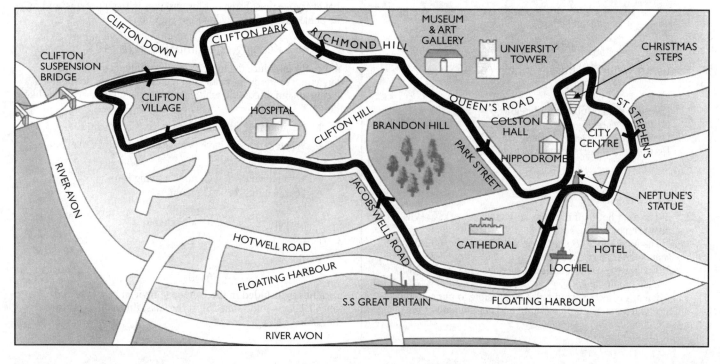

UNIT 4 ▶ Lawbreakers

▶ Lead-in (p. 56)

1 Ask students to look at the picture in pairs and try to match what is happening in the picture with the types of crime listed beneath it. Then check their answers:

vandalism - the man on the left writing graffiti on the wall with a spray can

burglary - the man escaping through a window on the left with goods he has stolen

robbery - two robbers running from the bank at the end of the street with bags of money

mugging - the hooded man in the centre of the picture threatening the woman with a knife as he snatches her handbag

shoplifting - the man leaving the TV shop with a TV under his coat

arson - the man leaving the burning building on the right with a can of fuel

stealing/theft - the man taking a radio cassette player from the car at the front right of the picture

Check that students know the name of the criminal in each case and that they are clear about what the different crimes entail (you *burgle* a house or other building; to *mug* someone is to attack them in a public place to get their money, etc.; *rob* and *steal*, see Study Box 1).

2 Allow students a few minutes to discuss the questions together before reporting back.

▶ Text 1 Seven banks a day are robbed in LA (p. 57)

2 1 It has far more (bank robberies) than any other American city.
  2 It was the last day that Los Angeles didn't have a bank robbery.
  3 The city has a large number of banks. They provide a lot of opportunities for robbers by staying open late in the evening and at weekends. They also tend to have a relaxed atmosphere.

3 Vocabulary

1	fond	9	surveillance
2	haul	10	makes a getaway
3	heads	11	freeway
4	league	12	heads
5	appreciative	13	squad
6	genteel	14	bandit
7	teller	15	doffs
8	pockets		

4 True/false

1 False. (The figure refers to business days and is, in any case, only an average.)
2 False. (*none of the machine-gun violence of the old movies.*)
3 True. (*Tellers have orders to hand over the money immediately.*)
4 False.(*'The banks believe, quite rightly,...' says one FBI man.*)
5 False. (*a smile in the direction of the cameras*)
6 False. (It was only the last single day without a robbery.)
7 True. (*the robber passes a stick-up note to a teller.*)
8 True. (*They are also very informal.*)

5 1 He has succeeded in committing so many robberies that he may have created a record. He also makes a habit of smiling at the cameras.
  2 To get money to buy drugs.
  3 They drive away (on to nearby freeways).

6 1 Because he has committed so many robberies and also, perhaps, because he makes the FBI look foolish.
  2 Perhaps 'This is a bank raid. Don't press the alarm or call for help. Give me $...'

Vocabulary included in the Language review: to head (line 13, 39), an awful lot (line 16), do business (line 20), to hand over (line 30), in the direction of (line 46).

▶ Focus on grammar 1 Modal verbs 2: obligation (p. 58)

Passage

you *have to* pay; you *should* allow; you *don't* usually *have to* pay; You *must* complete; you *needn't* send

Exercise 1

a	must	e	must
b	had to	f	have to
c	I've had to		
d	has to		

Exercise 2

a	needn't/don't have to	d	mustn't; needn't/don't have to
b	mustn't	e	mustn't
c	needn't/don't have to		

Exercise 3

a didn't need to go
b didn't need to buy *or* didn't have to buy
c needn't have written
d didn't need to have *or* didn't have to have
e needn't have damaged

Exercise 4

a You *mustn't* smoke in here.
b You ('ll) *have to* get a visa before you travel.
c I *needn't have done* all this cooking!
d You *must* go to bed now, children.
e You *needn't/don't have to* reserve a table.

▶ Focus on writing 1 Report (p.60)

Preparation

A good introduction would be for students to start by looking at the example report on page 126 of the Writing Bank. After they have read the question at the top, ask them what they notice about the **layout** of the report (heading and separate paragraphs with sub-headings). Then ask them to find out what the first and last paragraphs deal with.

Let students read the information for the task and ask questions to check that they have noted all the details. Remind them about the three key questions: What *kind* of writing do I have to do? *Who* is going to read it? (Accommodation Officer and other college authorities possibly), What is the *purpose*? These questions all affect the style, layout and organisation of the writing.

Give students plenty of time to discuss ideas for each section. Tell them that the more clearly they imagine the event, the easier the report will be to write and the more convincing it will be.

If possible pre-teach some of the useful language from the Writing Bank, page 126.

▶ Focus on listening 1 Crime report (p. 61)

Check that students understand the instructions before playing the tape.

The following numbers should be ticked: 3, 5, 7, 8, 10, 12. The following numbers should have a cross: 2, 6, 8. (Marks should be deducted for any numbers wrongly marked.)

When you are checking the answers make sure that students can say **why** the other numbers should not have ticks or crosses, since this is just as important to the exercise as marking the correct numbers.

Useful vocabulary: with the exception of; missing, break into (see Study Box 3), a handful of, a bargain price, get away (see Study Box 2), to trace, file, spanner, hammer, to jog a person's memory, a saloon car.

▶ Text 2 You're already well equipped to prevent crime (p. 62)

Multiple choice

1 D
2 B (*Many of us go around with the alarm switched off. We don't see ... We overlook ... We don't notice ...*)
3 C (the *stranger loitering ... the kids trying the car doors ... the sounds from the flat upstairs*)
4 C (*... you know more ... than the police ever could*)
5 B (*It's early days yet, but results so far are very encouraging.*)

Note: Not a: 'Wherever' is not the same as 'many of the areas'.

Vocabulary included in the Language review: keep a look-out.

▶ Communication activity Witness (p. 63)

Notes: This activity serves, among other things, to alert students to gaps in their knowledge of language for describing people. It creates a need for the relevant language and makes students especially receptive to subsequent teaching. For this reason, it is **not** a good idea to pre-teach special vocabulary or refer students to the Functions Bank beforehand.

The activity also provides useful practice for Part 2 of Paper 5 in the exam (Speaking).

1 Describing clothes

A	shorts	G	raincoat
B	skirt	H	collar
C	trousers (man) or slacks (woman)	I	blouse
D	sleeve	J	overalls
E	jacket	K	cap
F	T shirt	L	belt

Note: These are the main clothing items listed in the *Cambridge English Lexicon*, but you (or the students) may want to expand the list.

For extra practice, ask students to describe each other using the tenses in the examples.

3 Procedure

First explain how the activity will work orally. Then ask students to read the introduction and check that they understand exactly what to do.

Students usually need little if any help with the activity, but it is useful to monitor their progress and to note down any language gaps they have.

Make sure each pair has looked at the picture together before they change roles. Monitor the class as before.

At the end, discuss the results briefly and deal with any vocabulary problems the students had.

4 Who makes the best witness?

Again check that students understand the introduction before they start the pairwork. It is also a good idea to elicit one or two more examples like the one given before pairwork begins.

Refer students to the Functions Bank on page 111. Depending on your students' needs, you may want to deal with this language in greater depth.

Students could be asked to produce written comparisons for class or homework.

The main difference between the two groups was that the police remembered the two people's appearance very accurately but were less accurate in recalling what actually happened. In fact, they remembered **more** than what actually happened, with details that weren't there. The situation with the public was almost exactly the reverse.

These findings are the result of a real experiment!

▶ Focus on listening 2 Bad start to a honeymoon (p. 65)

Pre-check the word 'honeymoon'.

1 (To) the airport.
2 tickets

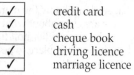

tickets	✓	credit card	✓
passports	✓	cash	
travellers' cheques		cheque book	✓
flight bag	✓	driving licence	
suitcases	✓	marriage licence	

3 Some friends.
4 Under a blanket.
5 Because his father is a senior policeman.
6 No.
7 A winter coat.
8 She works in a bank.
9 C (*They've managed to fix us up with another holiday, in Rhodes ...*)
10 A (*...things can only get better after this!, ... it's marvellous to be married.*)

▶ Text 3 Granny, 70, holds up a bank! (p. 66)

1 1 ✓ (she held a perfume spray in her pocket to look like a gun)
   2 ✓ (she describes herself as 'normally very timid')
   3 ✗ (we know how she travelled to the bank but not how she began the robbery)
   4 ✓ (she had large debts)
   5 ✗ (we know that she was led away by police but that's all)
   6 ✗

2 Encourage students to look for clues which help them to place the paragraphs. For example, *First ...* in paragraph D is logically followed by *Then...*, or *She added* in paragraph C logically follows *she said later.*

   1 B
   2 D
   3 A
   4 E
   5 C

3 3 She grabbed a customer as a hostage.
   5 Her hostage managed to overpower her.
   6 She was given a nine month prison sentence, suspended for a year.

4 1 False She had a pensioner's pass.
   2 True She used a walking stick.
   3 True She took a hostage by pretending to have a gun.
   4 True She had debts of £70,000.
   5 False She admitted assaulting the customer.
   6 False She apologised to the bank staff, not the judge.
   7 True She is normally timid.

5 Example answer

The robber was older; she wasn't a drug addict; she didn't use a stick-up note; she didn't make a getaway in a car; she also wasn't successful!

Vocabulary included in the Language review: hostage (line 3), turn out to be (line B), to bundle/a bundle (line 15), settle for (line 23), to sentence (to prison)/a sentence (line E), admit + ing (line E).

▶ Focus on grammar 2 Participles (p. 68)

Exercise 1

a	*inviting* place	d	*Bespectacled* widow
b	*working*	e	*stolen* chequebook
c	*built-in* burglar alarm		

Exercise 2

a	tiring	e	well-known	i	brightly-lit
b	ground	f	frightening	j	warning
c	long-lasting	g	helping		
d	worn	h	broken		

Exercise 3 (Example answers)

a	Crossing	e	Not knowing
b	Having worked	f	Having spent
c	Looking out of	g	Seeing
d	Waiting for	h	Having tried

Exercise 4

a (While) *unloading* the car after the holiday, we realised ...
b She rushed to answer the phone, *knowing* that it might be ...
c *Having taken* my name and address, the sergeant asked me ...
d *Not finding* anyone at home, she pushed a note ...
e *Having eaten* a three-course meal already, I had to refuse ...
f *Tearing* open the letter, he found ...
g *Thinking* that I had stolen the bag, the shop assistant called ...
h *Not being* used to the climate, I found it ...

▶ Focus on writing 2 Description (p. 70)

Preparation

Remind students about the three key questions to ask: **What? Who?** and **Why?** and check that they know exactly what to do.

It is useful to have a class planning session when students can discuss their appearance and clothes with each other and also check on any vocabulary they might need.

Point out that there is an example description of a person in the Writing Bank (though this has more detail than is needed for this task) and notes on useful language.

▶ Language review (p. 70)

1	C (1.46/47)	9	A (3.23)
2	B (1.20)	10	C (3E)
3	B (1.16)	11	A (3E)
4	D (1.13)	12	B (3B)
5	D (1.30)	13	A (2)
6	D (3.15)	14	C (Describing clothes)
7	B (3.3)	15	C (Study Box 2)
8	D (Study Box 1)		

▶ Lead-in (p. 72)

1

1	bottle	(perfume, vinegar)
2	tube	(toothpaste, glue)
3	box	(chocolates, matches)
4	bag	(apples, potatoes)
5	carton	(cream, orange juice)
6	jar	(instant coffee, honey)
7	packet	(cigarettes, envelopes)
8	tin	(soup, pineapple)

Note: Several of the items above can, of course, be bought in more than one type of container, for example, orange juice (bottle, carton), glue (tube, jar).

2 What is packaging for? (Example answers)

To protect the contents.
To give instructions for use.
To hold a definite amount.
To tell you what the contents are.
To make you want to buy the product.

The purpose of the task is not to find a number of 'right' answers but to discuss various issues concerned with packaging. For example:

How much packaging is unnecessary?
How much information on packaging is useful?
How much are we influenced by packaging in deciding what to buy?
What are the negative effects of packaging?

Discuss the results of the pairwork briefly before going on to Text 1.

Vocabulary included in the Language review: contain

▶ Text 1 A load of old rubbish? (p. 73)

It's better not to introduce the topic beforehand as this would defeat the purpose of Question 1.

As with previous examples of 'gapped text' questions, encourage students to look for clues to help them place the sentences correctly. These can be phrases like *high price* in sentence F, which matches with *£720 million*, or *My husband and I* in D, which matches with *a young professional couple*. They should also look for places where direct speech will fit.

1 C

2

1	B (example)	4	C	
2	F	5	E	
3	D	6	A	

3

1	snipped	5	a cheat	
2	fancy	6	dispose of	
3	economy	7	junk mail	
4	disposable	8	assortment	

4 (Example answers)

1 Because, unlike people today, she used to save packaging carefully to be used again.
2 Because it creates a lot of rubbish, which is expensive to dispose of.
3 Paper and food containers.
4 Because some of the materials it contains could be used again, and some use limited resources and are also difficult to dispose of.

Vocabulary included in the Language review: regard ... as (line 7), consist of (line 15)

Focus on grammar 1 Conditional 1 (p. 74)

Zero conditional

You may prefer to elicit suitable examples and focus on the **form** on the board, rather than have students reading through this section in the book.

Exercise 1

a   freezes
b   drop it in water
c   boils
d   lights/ignites
e   For example, don't water them
f   For example, eat too much

Exercise 2

1 e	3 f	5 i	7 j	9 g
2 h	4 a	6 c	8 d	10 b

Conditional 1

Again, you may prefer to present this section on the board rather than by asking students to read through the notes in the book.

Exercise 1

a   *I'll give* you a ring if I *need* any advice.
b   He *can only come* if the meeting *takes* place on a Friday.
c   If you *don't pass* the examination, *will you take* it again?
d   She*'ll just have to* take a taxi if she *misses* the train.
e   If you *go* to see him now, he*'ll be working*.
f   We*'ll lose* our way if we *don't keep* to the main road.
g   If the weather *is* sunny, we*'ll have brought* our umbrellas for nothing.
h   If you *don't speak* clearly, he *won't be able to* understand.

Exercise 2 (Example answers)

a   If you find 'Tibbles', you'll receive a reward of £25.
b   If you park there, you'll have to pay a fine of £50.
c   If you enter the photography competition, you'll have a chance of winning £1,000.
d   If you haven't got a visitor's pass, you won't be able to go in.
e   If you have two garments cleaned in this shop, you'll only have to pay for one of them.
f   If you drink the contents of that bottle, you'll die.

Other conditional link words

Exercise

a   unless
b   Suppose
c   as long as/provided (that)

Example answers

d   (that) the weather is good.
e   you lose your ticket.
f   they know where I am.
g   you pay me back in a month.

Focus on listening 1
The sweet, short life of products (p. 76)

A possible lead-in is to ask students to discuss (in pairs) how long they have had their cameras, bicycles, etc. Ask them to suggest what the life span of these products is and write their answers on the board.

Give students time to read the instructions and the questions, and check that they understand what to do and that there are no vocabulary problems.

1   A light bulb.
2   A new style, colour or extra improvements.
3   (The) fashion and car (industries).
4   The kitchen.

The Useful Life of Products (in years)			
Products	Useful life of product (manufacturer's estimate)	Actual time in use in the USA	Actual time used in underdeveloped countries
a Washing machines and irons	5	5	25
b Cars	11	2.2	40+
c bicycles	25	2	75
d Construction equipment	14	8	100+
e ships	30	15	80+
f Photographic equipment	35	11	50

Vocabulary included in the Language review: wear out, persuade someone to do something.

Other useful vocabulary: out of date, to cash in, scarce, to break down, to patch, to replace ... with, vital, to shrink.

Communication activity 1 Pollution (p. 77)

Note: This activity provides practice in describing a picture for Paper 5 in the examination (Speaking).

The students have their books closed. Explain the activity and make sure that students understand **what** they have to do and **how** they're going to do it.

Tell students who to work with and, if possible, rearrange seating so that students are facing each other. If this is not possible, ask them to mask their books so that their partner cannot see their picture.

Assign roles A and B in each pair and tell students which pages to turn to.

The students open their books and begin. Monitor the activity, making sure that students are describing their pictures in enough detail and that they are asking each other questions. Make sure too that one student in each pair is writing down a list of the differences they find.

Give help if necessary by supplying unknown vocabulary or by indicating an area of the picture that could be examined more closely.

If a pair finds five differences fairly quickly, they may prefer to go on and find as many more as they can **without** looking at the pictures. If they have taken more time to find five, remind them that they can now find the rest by comparing the two pictures.

Differences in A's picture (from left to right)

1   Man is smoking a cigar, not a cigarette.
2   Woman is spraying flowers with left hand.
3   There are only 4 rubbish bags, not 5.
4   Woman shopper has a shoulder bag, not a shopping bag.
5   Stripes on teenager's shirt are different.
6   No picture of a burger above the shop sign.
7   Traffic sign is different.
8   Car registration number is different.

Checking

Ask students to describe each difference accurately and establish relevant vocabulary from the list above.

Check other useful vocabulary illustrated in the picture, for example, window box, aerosol can, dustbin, pavement, kerb, radio-cassette player, exhaust fumes.

Ask students what examples of pollution they can see in the picture, for example, noise pollution (music and cars), air pollution (factory smoke, exhaust fumes and aerosol spray), litter.

▶ Text 2 Recycling (p. 78)

1 1 C (Section B)
   2 D (Section H – *almost impossible to separate for recycling*)
   3 D (Section I – *their deposit is returned, making the drinks cheaper*)
   4 B (Section K – *they are ground and remelted*)
   5 A (Section G – *imported paper can be cheaper when the pound is strong*)
   6 C (Section J – *Alcan will send you the address of your nearest collection centre*)

   7 A
   8 C
   9 C
   10 B

▶ Text 3 (p. 80) Friends of the Earth Trust Ltd.

2

1 True **and** false. (It's one aim but not the only one.)
2 False. (It's one danger, but there are many others.)
3 True. (*About half the world's animal and plant species could be extinct.*)
4 False. (Forests the size of Wales, not in Wales.)
5 False. (*New jobs would be created ...*)
6 True.
7 True **and** false. (Bicycles are recommended for short journeys.)
8 True. (*Cycleways should be built ...*)

Vocabulary included in the Language review: be/become aware of (line 3), to waste (line 6), resources (line 7), cut down (line 17), spend ... on (line 34).

▶ Focus on grammar 2 Conditional 2 (p. 81)

As in the previous grammar section, you may prefer to present the example(s) and form on the board.

Exercise 1

a Your uncle would really appreciate it if you *went* to see him.
b If she *made* more effort to help herself, I'd have more sympathy with her.
c Chris *wouldn't take* a day off work unless he *was/were* really ill.
d If you *knew* her as well as I do, you *wouldn't rely* on her at all!
e We'*d have* to reduce the price if we *wanted* to sell our house quickly.
f If electric cars *didn't have* such large batteries they'*d be* faster to drive.
g If you *called* the Fire Brigade, how long *would it take* them to arrive?
h I *wouldn't carry* your wallet around in your pocket if I *were* you.

Exercise 2

First ask students to say what's wrong about Martin's appearance.

long hair
unshaven
sunglasses
crooked tie
bulging pockets

Suggested answers

If he	straightened his tie, shaved/had a shave, took off his sunglasses, emptied his pockets,	, he'd ...

▶ Communication activity 2 Follow the country code (p. 82)

Ask students to suggest what the term Country Code means. Unless they can do this at once, remind them of the similar expression, Highway Code, and give one or two examples from it, such as: Look in your mirror before you overtake to make sure it's safe to do so. (You could elicit one or two more.) Ask what a *code* is (a list of rules).

Students can either perform the task individually and compare their answers afterwards, or work together from the start.

When checking the answers, ask students to explain their choices by describing what they can see in the pictures.

Keep your dogs under control.	3	Keep to public paths across farmland.	4
Help to keep all water clean.	8	Guard against all risk of fire.	1
Take your litter home.	7	Take special care on country roads.	10
Fasten all gates.	2	Protect wildlife, plants and trees.	9
Leave livestock, crops and machinery alone.	6	Use gates and stiles to cross fences, hedges and walls.	5

3 Example sentences

a If you left litter lying about, it would spoil the view for other people.
b If you didn't fasten gates behind you, cattle might escape.
c If you didn't keep to public paths across farmland, you might damage crops.
d If you drove carelessly on country roads, you might injure an animal.
e If you didn't use gates and stiles, you might damage fences, hedges or walls.

Vocabulary included in the Language review: under control, leave ... alone, keep to.

▶ Focus on writing Discussion (p. 83)

This is a fairly serious **discussion** topic but as it's in the form of an article it needs to appeal to the general reader.

Begin with three important questions: *What* am I writing about? (two separate issues here), *Who* am I writing for? (adult readers from different countries and situations), What is the *purpose*? (to make readers more aware and maybe to change their behaviour).

Work through the preparation phase, stage by stage, allowing the students plenty of oral practice. Monitor the work of groups and pairs.

1 At the end of stage 1, draw up a list of students' suggestions on the board so that there is a wide range of types of pollution for students to refer to.

2 Check students' ideas about who is responsible before they practise explaining causes.

3 Again, collate students' ideas on the effects of pollution, possible solutions and problems on the board before they practise orally using language from the tables.

▶ Focus on listening 2 (p. 84)

1 C
2 1 LD   5 PD (the most heavily used)
   2 S   6 N (Hadrian's Wall)
   3 PD   7 S
   4 PC (the most densely populated)   8 N

3

A 1   B 2   C 3   D 4
E X   F 6   G 5   H X
I X   J 7

Note: This part contains a number of words and phrases describing shapes, and it would be a good time to revise and practise these. There is a full list on pages 109–110 of the Functions Bank.

▶ Focus on grammar 3
Modal verbs 3: permission (p. 86)

1 Talking about permission

Exercise

1   a   public footpaths
     b   take a pram or pushchair ... take a dog which is not on a lead.
     c   go on horseback
     d   could

Practice

Note: You may also like to refer students to the Functions Bank, page 107, for other ways of asking for and giving permission.

2 Asking for and giving permission

Exercise 1 Example answers

a   Can I borrow your ruler for a minute?
     – No, (I'm sorry you can't,) because I'm using it.
b   May I come in?
     –Yes, of course.
c   Excuse me, I wonder if I could use your telephone? My car's broken down.
     – Yes, of course. Come in.
d   Excuse me. Could I (possibly) look at your map for a moment?
     – Yes, do.
e   Can I (Do you mind if I) go across your field?
     – No, you most certainly can't!
f   Could I drive your new car?
     – No, you can't!
g   Could I possibly interrupt for a second?
     – Yes, of course.
h   I wonder if I could possibly borrow £100 – just for two days?
     – No, I'm awfully sorry, but I'm rather hard up at the moment.

▶ Language review (p. 88)

1   B (Communic. activity 2)   9   B (3.3)
2   D (Communic. activity 2)   10   D (3.6)
3   A (Communic. activity 2)   11   C (1.15)
4   C (Listening 1)   12   B (Focus on grammar 3)
5   B (Listening 1; Study Box 1)   13   A (3.34)
6   D (Lead-in)   14   C (3.20)
7   C (Study Box 3)   15   D (1.7)
8   A (3.7)

UNIT 6 ▶ The shape of things to come

▶ Lead-in (p. 89)

You could begin by writing the names of some famous inventors on the board and asking students what they all have in common, and then what they invented. Examples: Alexander Graham Bell (telephone, 1876), Montgolfier brothers (hot-air balloon, 1783), Rudolph Diesel (diesel engine, 1895), King C. Gillette (safety razor, 1895).

1 Remind students of the ways of defining things and describing their use from Unit 1 (page 16) e.g. I think/Maybe *it's a thing that you use for ...ing.*

▶ Text 1 What's the big idea? (p. 90)

1   1 B   2 C

2   This is an example of the 'multiple matching' type of question in the examination. Encourage students to *scan* fairly quickly for the information they need and not to waste time wondering about words they don't understand.

1   B   7   B
2   D   8   E
3   E   9   D
4   A   10   C
5, 6 B, C   11, 12 D, E

3

1   came across   6   dummy
2   driven her almost out of her mind   7   draught
3   debut   8   dead
4   marketing strategy   9   portable
5   ingenious

Vocabulary included in the Language review: along (line 3)

▶ Focus on grammar 1
Talking about the future 1 (p. 92)

Exercise 1

a   are you going to wear/are you wearing
b   I'm having/going to have
c   I'm not taking
d   We are having/going to have
e   Are you doing/going to do
f   aren't you going
g   is playing
h   are you going to do

Exercise 2 (Example answers)

a   's going to be a storm.
b   is going to break
c   isn't going to bite me.
d   's going to be an accident.
e   're going to run out of
f   'm going to sneeze.
g   is going to be a draw.
h   isn't going to be a strike.

Exercise 3 (Example answers)

a   How *do we get* to Dover?
b   Which French port *do we travel to?*
c   What time do *we arrive* in Paris?
d   What *happens* on the first evening?
e   What *do we do* on Monday?
f   Where *do we go* on Tuesday?
g   What *do we see* in the afternoon?

h   When *do we leave* for Epernay?
i   What else *do we do* there?
j   What time *do we arrive* back in London?
k   Where *do we stop* during the trip?
l   Are there any extras that *we have to pay for*?

Note: If your students have made a lot of mistakes with prepositions in Exercise 3, it would be a good time to revise prepositions of time and place, for example:

at 6 o'clock, night, etc.
on Monday, Monday evening, etc.
in the afternoon, etc.
live *in*
arrive *in* (large city)
arrive *at* (smaller place)
travel *to*

▶ Focus on listening 1 Word processor mishaps (p. 93)

1 Word processing

it	would
takes	but
use	For
on	be
Then/Next/Later	with
of	for

1   You can correct mistakes and make changes without having to re-type your work. You can also store your work on a disk for future use.
2   You use a keyboard like a typewriter but the words appear on a screen rather than on paper. You also need a separate printer to print out the text, and disks.

2

		A	B	C	D
1	Profession	Cookery writer	Journalist	Novelist	TV Reporter
2	Make of machine	X	Astra	Rocket 22	X
3	What was lost	50 Recipes	an article	2 chapters	Script for a documentary

4

	A	B	C	D
A fault of the machine			✓	
The speaker's mistake	✓			
Someone else's mistake		✓		
Another reason (say what it was)				a burglary

5   A (Cookery writer)

Vocabulary included in the Language review: satisfied with, as far as I'm concerned, cut off (see also Study Box 2).

▶ Focus on writing 1 Instructions (p. 94)

Ask students to work in pairs and discuss the steps which the pictures show.

Check results and practise instructions for the first three pictures orally. Draw students' attention to the sequence markers and vocabulary under *Useful language*. If your students need more help, go through all the instructions orally first.

Example answer

First, lift the systems box carefully out of the carton and place it on a flat surface, removing the polystyrene packaging from the sides. Next, remove the polythene wrapping from the monitor and place the monitor in the groove on top of the systems box. Check that the power is switched off before connecting the monitor to the systems box by plugging in the power flex. After that, unwrap the keyboard and place it in front of the systems box. Finally, adjust the position of the monitor so that it is convenient for you to work at.

Vocabulary included in the Language review: plug in

▶ Focus on grammar 2
Sudden decisions, offers, suggestions, threats (p. 95)

Exercise 1 (Example answers)

a   Shall I open the window? (Offer)
b   I'll look it up in the dictionary. (Sudden decision)
c   I'll take it away from you. (Threat)
d   Shall I give it some water? (Offer/Suggestion)
e   I'll pay for it to be cleaned. (Promise)
f   Shall I see who it is? (Offer)
g   I'll clear it up. (Promise)
h   Shall I phone the Fire Brigade? (Suggestion)
i   I'll report you to the police! (Threat)
j   Shall I book a hotel for you? (Offer)

▶ Focus on listening 2 (p. 96) Life in the future

Give students time to read the instructions and questions, and check that these are understood before playing the tape.

1

	First group	Second group
space travel	✓	
robots	✓	
computers	✓	✓
nuclear weapons	✓	✓
overpopulation	✓	✓

	First group	Second group
test tube babies		
unemployment	✓	
future places for people to live	✓	✓
future forms of energy		
future forms of communication		✓

2   1   B
       2   C
       3   C
       4   D

Vocabulary included in the Language review: go wrong with.

▶ Focus on grammar 3
Talking about the future 2 (p. 97)

Exercise 4 (Example answers)

a   It's no use going then because the sale will have finished.
b   It's no good going to the bank then because it will have closed.
c   It's no good leaving at midnight because the last train will have left.
d   There's no point in getting there at midday because my train won't have arrived yet.
e   There's no point in phoning me on the 15th because I won't have taken the exam by then.

Exercise 5

a   I'll have heard the results
b   it will probably cause some damage
c   I'll be swimming
d   I'll give you a hand
e   we'll have been married
f   what do you think will happen
g   they'll just be getting up/they'll just have got up
h   What are you going to do/will you do
i   Will the builders have finished
j   I doubt if you will get home

▶ Communication activity 1 Role play (p. 100)

Note: This activity involves an information gap and, for this reason, it's best if the procedure is explained thoroughly before students start reading the instructions in the book.

Preparation

Students have their books closed. Explain to them that they are going to work in pairs, one as salesman/woman for an office equipment company, one as the boss of the company. Check 'office equipment' by asking what the company might sell (for example, desks, filing cabinets, typewriters, etc.).

Tell students that their instructions are on different pages of the book and that they should read them carefully before beginning the role play. They should not show their instructions to their partner!

Optional extra stage: You may like to make use of the Functions Bank for preliminary language practice. The following sections are relevant, but remind students of the need for a certain degree of formality between boss and employee: Agreeing/Disagreeing (pages 105-106); Making and Responding to Suggestions (page 107); Expressing Need and Use (page 108).

Decide which students should work in pairs and allot roles A and B. Tell A students to turn to page 100, B students to page 104. Students open their books. Check with individual pairs that they have understood their instructions before they begin.

An alternative approach is to ask all students with A and B roles to form two groups and discuss any problems before they begin. Again, check with each group to answer any questions before pairwork begins.

Role play

Monitor the role play unobtrusively and make a note of any language problems which arise. It is best not to interrupt or interfere unless absolutely necessary.

Feedback

Ask students to comment on the conversation they have had and the results. Deal with any language problems you have noted.

▶ Text 2 Super-watches (p. 101)

1   Give students time to discuss the questions and then check words for watch parts and ask students to report back on any interesting stories they have heard about their partner's watch.

a minute hand   c hour hand
b face   d strap

2   With this multiple matching question again remind students not to worry about every word but to scan the text for the information they need.

0	F (example)	6	C
1	B	7	A
2	G	8	E
3	D	9	A
4, 5 A, B			

Vocabulary included in the Language review: watch strap

▶ Communication activity 2 Describe and Draw (p. 102)

Preparation

Read through the introduction and instructions with the students and make sure they are understood.

If necessary, revise basic vocabulary for describing buildings – roof, chimney, windows, floors etc.

You may prefer to elicit the key language for expressing location and describing shape and put this on the board, rather than refer students to the Functions Bank.

Make sure students are facing each other and cannot see each other's books. Point out that basic shapes are required, not artistic masterpieces!

Pairwork

Monitor the activity carefully and be prepared to help students who have difficulties. Encourage them to ask and answer questions. Note any particular language problems which arise.

Feedback

At the end of each drawing phase, ask students to compare their pictures with the original and discuss any differences. Ask if there was any vocabulary which they felt they needed.

▶ Focus on writing 2 Description/discussion (p. 102)

Preparation

It's useful to have a planning stage during which students can make suggestions and pool their ideas. A good way of doing this is to arrange students in small groups of 3–5 to discuss possible developments. They should base their discussion on the topics listed for the middle paragraphs. Tell them to make notes and be prepared to report back to the rest of the class afterwards.

During the discussion, monitor, make suggestions if necessary and encourage students to use appropriate language for expressing opinions and making predictions about the future. For example:

I think/I don't think there'll be ...
I think telephones will probably have screens ...
People may retire at 35.

After this groupwork, ask students to report back. Write up interesting ideas and useful vocabulary on the board.

▶ Language review (p. 103)

1	D (Study Box 1)	9	A (Focus on grammar 3)
2	C (Focus on grammar 3)	10	B (Listening 1)
3	B (Listening 2)	11	A (Focus on writing 1)
4	D (Listening 1)	12	D (Unit 2 Study Box 2)
5	A (Listening 1, Study Box 2)	13	B (Unit 5 Study Box 1)
6	C (Focus on grammar 1)	14	B (Unit 3 Study Box 3)
7	C (2)	15	B (Unit 5 Study Box 2)
8	D (1)		

UNIT 7 ▶ Going the hard way

▶ Lead-in (p. 128)

1 The four pictures and their accompanying questions provide practice for the second part of Paper 5 in the exam (Speaking).

For questions 1 and 2, encourage students to make full use of the information in the pictures and to give detailed rather than general answers, as far as possible. Point out that it isn't necessary to know the exact word to describe something, as long as you can make the meaning clear.

Go through the answers to questions 1 and 2 for picture A, showing how much information can be used and helping with vocabulary as necessary. Then ask students in pairs or small groups of 3 or 4 to work together to answer the same questions for pictures B to D.

Example answer, picture A

The picture shows a man on skis in a snowy region. It could be the Arctic or the Antarctic. He's standing near a flag and throwing his arms up into the air. Behind him there's something which looks like a sledge with his equipment on it, probably. There doesn't seem to be anyone with him, apart from the photographer, that is!

He's completely covered up to protect himself from the cold. He's got a thick jacket and trousers on. His head is covered so that you can't even see his face. He's wearing gloves and boots.

For questions 3–6, encourage students to use the language of speculation rather than only the terms 'probably' or 'maybe'.

it	might			might	
he	could	be ...	he	could	have (done)
they	may	have ...		may	
he	he				be
it	seems + adjective		it	seems to	have
he	looks like + noun		he		
it			it	looks as if + clause	

Revise the language of speculation, using questions 3 and 4 as examples. Then ask the same pairs/groups as before to work out answers for questions 5 and 6.

Example answer, picture A (question 3)

The flag means that he must be British. He could have reached some special place for the first time. It can't be the top of a mountain because he wouldn't have a sledge with him then. It might be somewhere like the North Pole.

Example answer, picture A (question 4)

He seems to be shouting out in joy because he has achieved something which is very difficult to do. He might be saying 'I've done it! I've reached the North Pole.'

2 The completed table is as follows. (Note: The last line cannot be completed until students have read through the extracts in task 5.)

	Pictures A	Pictures B	Pictures C	Pictures D
1 Method of travel	skis	motorbike	bicycle	boat
2 Destination	North Pole	Africa	Australia	China
3 Stores list	c	a	d	b
4 Extract	iv	ii	i	iii

3 Example answers

a 5 gallon jerrycan of petrol
b gloves, radio, satellite relay kit, 200 kilos of food, rifle
c several novels, metal suitcase
d cycle spares

5 See the table above.

6

1 Perhaps because the village people had never seen Westerners before, so they were interested to meet and welcome them.
2 Learning how to handle the bikes in different conditions.
3 Examples: inner tubes (for tyres), chains, etc.
4 They spread (distributed) the load they were carrying so that it was well balanced.
5 Because he didn't want to travel on the well-known routes from England or Holland, and there was a convenient boat from Athens which he could take on his way to the Suez Canal.
6 A steamer – a ship which is driven by steam power.
7 Difficult, 'a formidable major hurdle'.
8 Intense cold, tiredness, poor visibility, loss of radio contact with people who could help him, the fact that his compass wasn't working.
9 He wanted to be the first person to go there alone on foot.

Vocabulary included in the Language review: a load/to load (extract ii), spare (extract ii).

▶ Text 1 Freezing! (p. 130)

This first task encourages students to get a general idea of the story before they attempt to place the missing sections.

1 Example answers

1 The freezing temperatures.
2 He collapsed in the snow.
3 An Algerian man helped them.

2

0	F (example)	3	B
1	C	4	G
2	D	5	A

3

1 False (they had a tent)
2 True (*wearing every article of clothing we had with us*)
3 True (*he fell off his bicycle on to the snow*)
4 False (he *worked to bring his companion round*)
5 False (*he was clearly in danger*)
6 True (*before he had a chance to say anything*)
7 False (*David was aware of somebody approaching*)
8 True (David was *convinced that Rick would have died if it hadn't been for that man*)

Vocabulary included in the Language review: wrap up (line 9), bring (a person) round (line 23+ Study Box 3), response (line 25), take control of (line 39), *make an effort* (line 44)

▶ Focus on listening 1 Overland to Australia (p. 132)

Allow students time to read through the eight questions and to ask anything they might want to. Point out that question 2 refers to countries passed through *more than once*.

1	D	5	A, C, E
2	C, D, E	6	B, C, D
3	D, F, I	7	C
4	C	8	D

▶ Text 2 Trisha Greenhalgh (p. 132)

1

1　They had to cross a narrow bridge over a pond.
2　Mat rode straight over but Trisha stopped because she was afraid that she might fall in.
3　Mat left Trisha to overcome her fear alone and, in the end, she did.

Note: You may prefer to do the vocabulary matching exercise next if your students need more help.

2

1　B (*nothing to stop us falling ... if we overbalanced*)
2　D (*If I slip, I'll be in there ...*)
3　A (*There's nothing to it.*)
4　B (*he would give me at least an hour before coming to help.*)
5　C (*To remain stationary ... was suicide*)

3

1　blazing　　　6　bog
2　stifling　　　7　yelled
3　rickety　　　8　sickly
4　stagnant　　　9　stationary
5　sleepers　　　10　obstacles

Vocabulary included in the Language review: steam/to steam (line 10), What's up? (line 17), to slip (line 20), nothing to it (line 22), sweat/to sweat (line 34).

▶ Focus on grammar 1 The gerund (p. 134)

1 Gerunds after prepositions

Exercise 1

a　by　　　　d　of
b　before　　e　without
c　after

Exercise 2

a　*of* earning/making　　e　*on* paying (for)
b　*without* asking/getting　f　*with* working
c　*for* cutting　　　　　g　*from* joining/working in, etc.
d　*at* remembering　　　h　*in* getting/finding, etc.

Exercise 3 (Example answers)

a　paying it
b　riding horses
c　taking some family photos, etc.
d　looking after kids/youngsters, etc.

2 Gerunds after verbs

Exercise 1

a　3　　　e　2
b　5　　　f　8
c　4　　　g　1
d　7　　　h　6

Exercise 2 (Example answers)

a　going to the cinema so often
b　ironing
c　stroking them
d　falling off from time to time
e　whistling
f　working underground all day
g　reading it
h　stealing the money
i　looking it up in the directory
j　making it sound an attractive place to visit.

▶ Communication activity Quiz (p. 136)

It might be helpful to pre-teach *redundancy, redundancy pay* and *pay rise* to help students understand question 12.

Read through the introduction with the class and make sure they understand why the quiz was prepared, but don't read through the questions with them.

The activity is in four parts:

1　Students work through the questions individually, giving true answers. The teacher should go round to help with any comprehension problems.

2　Students compare their answers and discuss them. This stage should be fairly brief (maximum 5 minutes).

3　Students work in pairs to decide which answers should earn top marks. They should make a separate note of these. The teacher should make sure they understand the instructions first.

You may like to have a brief feedback stage where students report back their selected answers and say why they have chosen them.

4　Students then turn to the answer, page 228, and see whether they chose the right answers for the right reasons.

A further feedback stage may follow if there are any language points which the teacher has noted and would like to draw the students' attention to.

▶ Text 3 The call of the wild (p. 138)

This is another version of the 'gapped text' exam question and, as before, the best approach is to read through the text quickly, forming a general impression of the topic for each section, before attempting to place the headings.

1

0　D (example)　　4　B
1　G　　　　　　5　H
2　I　　　　　　6　E
3　A　　　　　　7　C

2

1　delicacy　　　6　wriggle
2　twig　　　　7　insulation
3　paralysed　　8　sturdy
4　hammering　　9　nomads
5　excruciating　10　hostile

▶ Focus on grammar 2 The past perfect (p. 139)

Exercise 1

a　my body had become
b　I'd run up
c　he had done
d　we had been riding

Form

Present perfect simple	Present perfect continuous
Had / Hadn't + past participle	Had / Hadn't + been + present participle

Meaning

a　The police didn't make any arrests because the thieves *had already left*.
b　If we used the past simple for both actions, it would mean that the thieves left *at the moment* when the police arrived. The numbers would reverse in that case.

a　were (2)　　had done (1)

b　had been riding (1)　　came (2)

Exercise 2

1	had just finished	11	had been dreaming
2	rang	12	decided
3	went	13	had mistaken
4	had told	14	noticed
5	opened	15	examined
6	saw	16	realised
7	had heard	17	had pushed
8	had looked	18	had never seen
9	shut	19	began
10	began		

Exercise 3

a The examiner said that he hoped we had read the instructions carefully.

b She explained that she wasn't sure she had found the answer to (my) question though she had spent a week thinking about it.

c He said he couldn't shake hands with me because his hands were oily and explained that he had been working on his car.

▶ Focus on listening 2 (p. 141)

Optional introduction

Write the headline from the Lead-in ('My lone walk to the North Pole') on the board and ask students to recall what they can about: the traveller's appearance, his method of travel, his equipment. (*Note:* They can turn to the picture on page 128 if their memories need jogging.)

Ask them what particular problems he mentioned in the short extract from a newspaper article. Elicit: poor visibility, radio and compass not working, feeling cold, tired, confused.

Ask the reason he gave for making the journey.

Ask what other methods of travel there are in the Arctic. Pre-teach: dog teams, snowmobiles, air support.

True/false

1 True.
2 False. (*I cracked three ribs and I gave up, I achieved about three-quarters of the distance*)
3 True. (*everyone said ... I would be dead in six days...*)
4 False. (*every minute I hated it*)
5 True. (*it was something that I had to get back to*)
6 False.
7 False. (He knew he was going through a migration route for polar bears, and he put Mars bars out at night because of that.)
8 True. (*I heard this rustling and this polar bear was after the Mars bar*)
9 False. (*I shot a round through the floor just to scare it*)
10 True. (*It really upset me ... It was a shame because they're such beautiful animals*)

▶ Focus on writing 1 Formal letter 1 (p. 142)

1 Layout

Tell students to draw a large rectangle on a piece of paper and to place the information on it *without* referring to the Writing Bank. Then ask them to check their layout against the example letter in the Writing Bank (page 114) and to complete the letter in their books correctly. Note any mistakes students make at the first stage and remind them about key features of layout e.g. never to put their name before their address.

When this task has been completed and discussed, ask students to read the letter silently and to say what information each paragraph gives (for example, paragraph 1 gives the reason for writing, with necessary information about which advertisement is being referred to).

Draw students' attention to useful phrases such as 'I was very interested in...', 'the advertisement in today's edition of ...', 'I look forward to hearing from you.'

3–4 Style

Unsuitable features of style include:

1 **Abbreviations:** for example, ad.
2 **Colloquial expressions and slang:** for example, fun, come along, About myself, I couldn't stand, a bit of money, I didn't stick ..., come in handy, great, call in for a chat.
3 **Ending:** 'Yours' is only suitable in a personal letter.
4 **General:** The letter is too casual in its approach. The writer doesn't seem to think it's necessary to 'sell' himself in the right way, and he isn't polite enough. (Ask students to compare this letter with the previous one.)

5 Writing task: Formal letter Part 1

This question introduces Part 1 of the Writing paper in the First Certificate exam. Give students time to read through the instructions and the advertisement, then tell them to cover the page and check to see how many of the details they can remember. Finally, ask them to underline all the key points they need to include.

Remind students of the importance of making a plan and checking that they have included all the necessary points before they begin writing the final letter.

▶ Focus on writing Formal letter 2 (p. 144)

1 Describing objects

A	(a saddle)	It's made of leather (the stirrups are made of steel).
B	(a record)	It's circular and made of plastic.
C	(a sweater)	It's made of wool/nylon/cotton etc. and it's spotted. The collar and sleeves are plain.
D	(a tie)	It's made of silk/cotton etc. and it's striped.
E	(a set square)	It's triangular and made of plastic.
F	(a table cloth)	It's square or rectangular and made of checked cotton or linen.
G	(a mirror)	It's oval and made of glass.
H	(a chest of drawers)	It's rectangular and made of wood.

2

long	short	wide	narrow	expensive	cheap
hard	soft	full	empty	enormous	tiny
heavy	light	sharp	blunt	curved	straight
thick	thin	tight	loose	dark (of colours)	light/pale
smooth	rough	hollow	solid		dull bright (of colours)

3 Writing task

This is a suitable task for homework. Remind students of the importance of thinking about the *purpose* of the letter and the intended *reader*, and of including *all* the points in the question and in the notes for the plan. You could revise *strap, buckle, handle* and *catch* from Unit 1 and any other relevant vocabulary students might need. You may also find it useful to revise the layout of formal letters briefly beforehand.

Language review (p. 145)

▶ 1	C (Lead-in 5ii)	9	D (1.38)
2	D (Lead-in 5ii)	10	C (2.20)
3	C (Focus on grammar 2)	11	A (2.17)
4	B (1.42)	12	B (2.34)
5	A (1.8)	13	A (2.22)
6	D (1.24)	14	B (2.10)
7	C (1.22; Study Box 3)	15	D (Focus on grammar 1)
8	B (Focus on grammar 1)		

▶ Odd man out (p. 146)

Suggested answers

1 *tram* – the others are kinds of boats
   or *yacht* – not normally public transport
2 *tractor* – the only one with an engine
   or *sledge* – hasn't got wheels
3 *car* – a private vehicle, not a commercial one
4 *taxi* – not public transport/doesn't have a fixed route
5 *runway* – part of an airport; the others are to do with rail transport.
6 *conductor* – doesn't have control of a vehicle
   or *cyclist* – his or her vehicle has no engine
7 *platform* – part of a station; the others are to do with ships
8 *station* – the others are to do with bus transport
9 *goat* – the only animal not used to pull vehicles
10 *Cairo* – not a sea port

Notes: There may well be other possible answers, and, if these are satisfactorily argued by students, they should of course be accepted.

All the vocabulary from this exercise and others like it in the book is included in the *Cambridge English Lexicon*, a word list used by those who prepare Cambridge examination materials.

Take the opportunity to revise and expand students' topic vocabulary by checking the meaning of all the items and explaining/illustrating those they don't know.

UNIT 8 ▶ Family life

▶ Lead-in (p. 147)

1 The two photographs provide further practice for the Picture Conversation part of Paper 5 (Speaking) in the examination.

A good way of making this a more interesting activity, and of providing useful practice in asking questions, is to follow the procedure for the 'Witness' communication activity in Unit 4.

Students work in pairs: Student A studies the first picture for 30–60 seconds and then closes the book. Student B then asks questions about the picture to see how much detail Student A remembers. The procedure is then reversed as Student B studies the second picture and is questioned in turn.

Afterwards, ask pairs to report back on any mistakes or omissions that were made, and give students the chance to ask for specific vocabulary items that they want to know. Take the opportunity to revise vocabulary relating to appearance and clothing, as necessary.

3 Questionnaire

Allow students time to read through the 12 statements and to ask any questions they may have before they start. The following may need checking/explanation:

1 financial support
2 the family budget
3 to share *fairly*
8 to have the last word
12 to respect a person's wishes (*Note:* The meaning here is probably 'to consider seriously, but not necessarily to follow'.)

When students have finished discussing their answers in pairs, open up a class discussion, asking students to give reasons for their opinions.

Vocabulary included in the Language review: to share *between* two people (*among* more than two).

▶ Text 1 Scruff Justice (p. 148)

You could begin with a brief discussion on the subject of tidiness, e.g. Who in the class is extremely tidy and who is untidy; Is tidiness important? – Why?/Why not?; What's the problem about an untidy desk? How do you keep your lesson notes and homework tidy? How do you encourage children to be tidy? etc.

1 Example answer

Simon refused to tidy his room and then locked himself in the garden shed so his mother called the police.

4 1 sharp
   2 bound over
   3 puts on a brave face
   4 budge
   5 a gulf
   6 worn down
   7 chores
   8 get it straight
   9 disorderly behaviour

5 1 C
   2 B
   3 C
   4 A
   5 D

Vocabulary included in the Language review: regret + ing

▶ Focus on grammar 1 The infinitive (p. 150)

Exercise 1 (Example answers)

a   to lose weight
b   to design our house
c   to report the burglary
d   to mend the washing machine
e   to tell him about my headaches
f   to put out the fire
g   to see the world
h   To win the match

Exercise 2

a   simple to use
b   disappointed to hear
c   anxious to know
d   certain to be
e   hard to believe
f   delighted to meet
g   amazed to see
h   important to check

Exercise 3 (Example answers)

a   to lift
b   to make an omelette
c   to take off/land
d   to sail
e   to read the notice
f   to take your driving test

Exercise 4 (Example answers)

a   persuade him to
b   prefer to
c   happen to
d   remind me to
e   forbade me to
f   afford to
g   advised me to
h   want/hope to
i   help you to
j   told you not to

Exercise 1

1   worrying
2   to spend
3   having
4   to stay
5   to look after
6   taking
7   to be
8   to arrange
9   combining
10 running
11 bringing up
12 to get
13 to buy
14 driving
15 get
16 to take
17 to get
18 travelling
19 staying
20 to get

▶ Communication activity (p. 153)

Follow the procedure for the similar communication activity in Unit 5 (page 20).

This time students should be able to find all ten differences without looking at the pictures together.

Differences

1   Flag (A: horizontal stripes; B: vertical stripes)
2   Shells on sandcastle (A: two; B: one)
3   Bucket next to man (A: upright; B: upside down)
4   Swimsuit (A: green with white spots; B: white with green spots)
5   Object near woman's foot (A: crab; B: starfish)
6   Book cover (A: heart shape; B: triangle)
7   Bottle (A: behind deckchair; B: beside deckchair)
8   Ship (A: pointing to the right; B: pointing to the left)
9   Bucket next to man (larger in picture B)
10 Glasses on picnic hamper (A: sunglasses; B: ordinary glasses)

Checking

Ask students to describe each difference accurately and check/teach the necessary vocabulary.

Check/teach any other useful vocabulary (for example, spade, yacht, beachball)

▶ Focus on listening 1 Children speaking (p. 153)

Give students time to read the instructions and the information given in the table. Check vocabulary as necessary (for example, *pocket money, punishment, lay the table, wipe up, a smack*).

	Age	Brothers/Sisters	Pocket Money	Spends Pocket money on	Help in the house	Punishment	Bed Time Earliest	Bed Time Latest
First child	9	2 brothers	£3.50	sweets	washing up and laying the table	gets sent to bed or gets a smack	9.30pm	11pm
Second child	7	1 brother 1 sister	50p	sweets	washing up, dusting, wiping up and putting things away	gets sent to bed	8 or 9pm	10pm
Third child	8	(none)	£1-£2	toys	lay the table and bring the knives and forks	gets a smack	8pm	11pm

Discussion points

1   Ask students to report back about what their partner said.
2   Open up a class discussion and invite as many opinions as possible.

▶ Text 2 Working mothers: what children say (p. 154)

With 'multiple matching' questions like this one it's important to read through the texts first so that you have a general idea of what they're about before you try to answer the question. To encourage this approach, ask students to skim each text fairly quickly to find out each child's opinion. Check answers before proceeding.

1   1 A   6 C
    2 B   7 D
    3 C   8 B
    4 D   9 C
    5 B   10 A

2   1 A   4 B
    2 C   5 A
    3 C   6 B

3   1 loads   4 told off
    2 mow   5 swap
    3 get round to

Vocabulary included in the Language review: make friends (A,16), get in the way (A,22), initial (A,31), wear off (A,31), trust (A,33), however (much) (A,36), fair (B,76)

▶ Focus on grammar 2 Reporting statements (p. 156)

Exercise 2

a   His wife complained that he never lifted a finger to help her.
b   My father promised that he would give me a hand with my homework that evening.
c   I explained that I was late because the bus had broken down.
d   My friend admitted that he had had an accident with my car.
e   The teacher argued that John ought to go first because he was the youngest.

Exercise 3

a   The interviewer asked him to shut the door.
b   My mother reminded me to switch off the fire.
c   The receptionist invited me to sit down and wait.
d   My friend advised me to lie down.
e   My boss forbade me to tell anyone about the product.
f   The gunman warned them not to move or he would shoot.
g   Some friends of mine recommended me to stay at the Imperial Hotel (if I could).

Exercise 4 (Suggested answers)

a   to sit in
b   that his car was in a
c   to play
d   that I had passed
e   not to make
f   to drive carefully
g   to feed
h   to try
i   that the library was/would be
j   not to go to Morocco in July

Focus on writing 1 (Part 1) Informal letter (p. 158)

Remind students how important it is to read the question carefully, to follow the instructions exactly and to include all the necessary information.

The more natural and realistic the letter sounds, the more successful it is likely to be. Suggest that if students don't have a real English friend they can imagine writing to, they should 'invent' one (deciding if they're male or female, how old they are, what their interests and occupation are, and so on).

Remind students to look at the example informal letter and the notes in the Writing Bank. If there is time, it would be useful to allow students to plan and produce a rough draft of their letter in class so that this can be checked.

Focus on listening 2 Single-parent family (p. 159)

Give students time to read through the questions and to ask any questions they may have before beginning the exercise.

1 True/false

1   False. (They separated 3 years ago.)
2   True. (a 13-year-old daughter and a 5-year-old son)
3   True. (*a very good supportive group of women friends* who *share the child care*)
4   False. (her mother-*in-law*)
5   True.
6   False. (He's in quite good health, so she only needs to visit him once every four weekends to see if he's OK.)
7   True. ('I get some help. I don't think it's enough really. I think ... fathers get off rather lightly.')
8   False. (They see him once a week.)
9   women
10 6 months
11 nothing
12 independent

2 Discussion points

These can be discussed in pairs, small groups, or by the class as a whole. You might even like students to give answers in writing, for homework, following the discussion.

Vocabulary included in the Language review: mind + ing

Focus on grammar 3
Comparatives: The ... the ... (p. 160)

Exercise 2 (Example answers)

a   *The more* exercise you take, *the fitter* you will become.
b   *The bigger* the car, *the more expensive* it is to hire.
c   *The more slowly* you speak, *the easier* it is for me to understand.
d   *The more* you study, *the greater (the)* chance you will have in the exam.
e   *The better* I get to know him, *the less* I like him, I'm sorry to say.
f   *The more frightening* the film, *the more* he enjoys it.
g   *The sharper* the knife, *the easier* it is to cut with.
h   *The longer* I stayed away, *the more homesick* I felt.

Exercise 3 (Example answers)

a   The more I earn, the happier I'll be. *or* The more money you have, the less contented you'll be.
b   The older you get, the wiser you become.

Focus on writing 2 Narrative (p. 161)

Ask students to study the example narrative in the Writing Bank (page 122). You could give them a time limit (e.g. 5 minutes) and then see how many of the key points they can remember.

1   See Writing Bank (page 122).

2   If there is time it would be useful for students to begin their planning in class. When they've decided on the stages and the beginning and ending, they could discuss these with a partner and/or the teacher.

Language review (p. 162)

1   C (1; 2D148)
2   D (2, A22)
3   B (2, A36)
4   A (Study Box 2)
5   C (Focus on grammar 1)
6   B (2, A31)
7   D (2, B76)
8   C (2, A16)
9   A (2,A31)
10 B (Focus on grammar 1)
11 A (2, A33)
12 D (Focus on grammar 1)
13 B (Focus on grammar 1)
14 D (Lead-in 3.5)
15 C (Listening 2)

UNIT 9 ▶ Looking after yourself

▶ Lead-in What is health? (p. 163)

Questionnaire

Ask the students to read through the 14 statements fairly quickly and to tell you if there are any words or expressions which they don't understand.

Draw their attention to 'out of breath', 'hardly ever' and 'a mild stomach upset' and check understanding.

When everyone has chosen their five statements (and ticked the first column), ask them to compare their results with one or (preferably) two other students and to write **their** results in the second column. Encourage them to discuss their reasons and to ask each other questions.

Feedback

Rather than work through all the students or all the statements, which can kill the interest in the topic, concentrate on common or uncommon answers:

Ask which numbers were chosen by all the members of each group, and see if there is any agreement across the class. If there is, do reasons correspond too?

Ask which numbers were only chosen by one member of each group and ask for reasons.

Passages

Allow students time to read each passage silently. At this stage, you may like to ask a student who has chosen one or more of the numbers mentioned to read a passage aloud. This skill is no longer tested in the examination, however.

Discuss the points raised. For example:

(Passage 1) How could you be fit and still be unhealthy?
(Passage 2) Why is it that doctors can do little to help us to be healthy?
(Passage 3) Is it worth living to be very old if you don't enjoy life?
(Passage 4) What can we do to encourage positive health?

Vocabulary included in the Language review: out of breath, hardly ever, suffer from, a mild cold.

▶ Text 1 (p. 164)

You could begin by asking students to write down three healthy and three unhealthy foods that they eat, and discussing these briefly.

Note: Ask the students to read and answer the True/false questions before they read Text 1. This provides a strong motivation to read the text in order to see if they were right or not. Discuss answers briefly (without judging them right or wrong) before students read the text.

1–2

1 True (*if you go on eating ... your health will suffer.*)
2 True (*The tendency to put on weight ... runs in families.*)
3 True (*Your upbringing shapes some basic attitudes ... a sweet tooth.*)
4 False (*You're more likely to put on weight ... if you're a woman.*)
5 False (*We eat about twice as much protein as we need.*)
6 True (*It is a waste of time and money to take vitamin pills.*)
7 False (*Don't make the mistake of thinking ... energetic.*)
8 False (*Food with plenty of fibre ... too many calories.*)

3

This is an example of another type of the 'multiple matching' question. As with all multiple matching questions, it's important for students to read the text first to form a general impression of what each section is about.

1 G 4 F
2 E 5 A
3 D 6 B

4

1 efficient 6 inherit
2 extracting 7 determine
3 huge 8 upbringing
4 cope 9 nibble
5 eventually 10 alter

5 Describing food

Spicy	Bitter	Salty	Sweet	Sour	Greasy	Creamy
curry	olives	peanuts	honey	lemon	fish and	butter
	beer	anchovies	ice cream	vinegar	chips	ice cream
	almonds	crisps	peaches	grapefruit	sausages	yoghurt
	coffee		bananas			onion soup
	(black)					

Note: Tastes differ! Other classifications are possible, within reason.

Optional writing exercise

Write two paragraphs, one describing your favourite dish and one describing the dish you think is most unpleasant.

Vocabulary included in the Language review: (The section number of the text is given in brackets) not *counting* (1), *put on* weight (2), raw (3), varied (4), unless (4), in comparison *with* (6).

▶ Focus on listening 1 Old wives' tales? (p. 166)

It is helpful to give an example of an old wives' tale that students might be familiar with. Check that students are quite clear about the meaning of this phrase before proceeding.

Ask students to guess whether the five old wives' tales given are true, partly true, or false, and to discuss their opinions with one or two other students. Don't confirm or deny their answers at this stage!

Check the meaning of tales 1 and 4 in particular and explain if necessary. Tale 1: Eating an apple every day will keep you healthy so that you don't need to see a doctor. Tale 4: Have plenty to eat when you've got a cold but don't eat anything if you've got a high temperature.

1

1 Partly true (an exaggeration).
2 False (dangerous for old people and babies).
3 False (no evidence).
4 True.
5 True (contains Vitamin A, which enables the eye to adapt to the dark).

3

1 An orange.
2 Old people and babies.
3 He fell into a freezing river (during the spring thaw).
4 To drink plenty of liquid (to replace fluid lost through sweating).
5 Green beans, milk, butter, fish oils.

▶ Focus on grammar 1 Expressing quantity (p. 167)

Countable and uncountable nouns

Exercise 1

Countable		Uncountable	
biscuit	coin	rice	money
vitamin	chair	spaghetti	blood
apple	programme	crockery	information
snack	journey	news	weather
plate		furniture	travel
		music	

Exercise 2

cheese	(i)	complete cake of food
	(ii)	food substance
time	(i)	an occasion
	(ii)	the passing of days etc.
wood	(i)	a group of trees
	(ii)	material
hair	(i)	a single piece of hair
	(ii)	all the hairs on one's head
iron	(i)	an instrument for smoothing clothes
	(ii)	material
tin	(i)	a container
	(ii)	material
exercise	(i)	an activity to train the body
	(ii)	activity in general
skin	(i)	an animal hide
	(ii)	the substance which covers the body

Much/many, a lot of

Exercise 1

Countable	Uncountable	Both	
too few	too much	a lot of	no ... at all
very many	a large amount of	hardly any	plenty of
a great many	very little	not enough	a lack of
a large number of	a great deal of		

Exercise 2

a	how much	f	number
b	little	g	plenty of/a lot of
c	no applause at all	h	deal of
d	lack	i	hardly any/very little
e	not enough/too few	j	many

As ... as

Exercise

A Bristol has twice as many inhabitants as Southampton.
B The first camera costs three times as much as the second.
C It's nearly twice as hot in Athens today as it is in London.
D The trains from London to Brighton are three times as frequent as those from London to Swansea.
E Mount Everest is more than six times as high as Ben Nevis.
F Concorde is ten times as fast as a BMW.

▶ Focus on writing 1 Article (p. 169)

1 As well as purpose, remind students to think about the age and interests of the likely readers.

2 If your students are all from the same country or if you can divide the class easily into country groupings, it would be useful to have a brainstorming session here so that as many ideas as possible are generated.

4 If there is time, revise key features of articles from the Writing Bank and provide some oral practice in the language for describing taste and smell e.g. taste/smell + adjective; taste/smell like + noun (See Functions Bank p. 110).

▶ Communication activity
The Laughing Cook restaurant (p. 170)

Preparation

Decide beforehand which roles students will have. The role of A is probably most suitable for stronger students. If the class doesn't divide evenly into threes, the extra one or two students can act as observers. They should be told privately that they will be asked to report back on what they've seen.

Let students read the introduction and menu on page 170 (tell them not to turn to the instructions for each role yet). Check that they know what they have to do and answer any questions about vocabulary they may want to ask.

Tell each student whether he/she is A, B or Waiter.

Ask all the waiters to form a group at the side of the class for a few minutes. They should read and discuss their instructions. Tell them privately to decide what to say when they go to take an order and also to discuss what they can say in order to persuade the customers to order the three dishes which the chef wants to get rid of. (You can suggest they look at the Functions Bank on pages 106 -7.)

Ask the A and B students to sit together as if they were in a restaurant. This will work much better if they can sit facing each other across a table, even if it means a bit of moving about to achieve the arrangement. Ask them to turn to their instructions and read them but **not** to show each other!

Role play

Check that each pair has decided on their relationship and then let the activity begin.

Allow about 5 minutes' conversation before telling the waiters to approach their customers. Meanwhile tour round and listen in, making your presence felt as little as possible. Note down any language difficulties.

Feedback

As each group finishes, let them look at each other's instructions. When everyone has finished, ask each group to report back briefly on what dishes were chosen and why. Ask them to say how persuasive A and the Waiter were, and ask any observers for their comments.

(Optional) Refer students to the Functions Bank on page 106 -107and practise as necessary. Deal with any language difficulties that you have noted.

▶ Focus on grammar 2 Reported questions (p. 171)

Questions with question words

'Excuse me, *where is the post office?*'
She asked me how my parents *were*.
They wanted to know who I *had gone home with*.

Exercise 1

a ... how much I earned.
b ... where I had bought my watch.
c ... how many kilos I had lost.
d ... when I was coming/going to stay with her.
e ... why she wouldn't marry him.
f ... who on earth had given him my address.

I asked you if you *liked jazz*.
He asked if he *could use the telephone*.

Questions without question words

Exercise 1

    a   ... if I had (got) change of a £5 note.
    b   ... if I had seen Tim that day.
    c   ... would be at home that weekend.
    d   ... if my wife spoke any Portuguese.
    e   ... if I had telephoned her the previous night.
    f   ... if I could lend him £1 till the following day.

Exercise 3

    a   ... what the capital of Australia is?
    b   ... what the language spoken in Holland is?
    c   ... what the unit of currency in Japan is?
    d   ... who the President of France is?
    e   ... where the nearest bank is?
    f   ... when the next First Certificate examination is/will be?
    g   ... what time it is?
    h   ... where the last Olympic Games were (held)?
    i   ... what the word 'dawn' means?
    j   ... how long the course lasts?

▶ Focus on listening 2 (p. 173)

Explain that students are going to hear part of a talk about First Aid. Give them time to read through the questions and ask about any vocabulary they don't know.

Multiple choice

1   D   (One afternoon a week for a total of 20 hours.)
2   A   (You can be a more effective first aider if you're prepared ... to do some extra practice at home.)
3   C   (He was purple.)
4   D   (Lying across the chair ... facing the floor)
5   C   (sometimes people get terrified in this kind of situation.)
6   A   (something ... blocking his airway)
7   D   (They took him off anyway because he needed to be medically examined.)
8   B   (You've got to recognise what sort of situation it is and, if it's an emergency, act very, very quickly.)

▶ Text 2 Cuts, bruises, bites, burns (p. 174)

A possible lead-in would be to draw a cross (like the Red Cross symbol) on the board and ask students what it would mean if they found that sign in red on a white box. When would they need to use the contents of the box and why? Elicit from the students some names of minor injuries (for example, *nose bleed, black eye, twisted ankle*) and ask what treatments they would recommend.

1   1   Plaster and bandage are not minor injuries.
        2   (From left to right) burn, scald, plaster, bruise, cut, bandage, bite (but bee's/wasp's *sting*), graze.

2 Allow 2–3 minutes' reading time and then ask students to answer the questions.

    1   D   Check why the other options are wrong:
        A   – It is not always necessary for a doctor to come;
        B   – We *know* what causes minor illnesses;
        C   – Not always, for example if the patient has been knocked out.
    2   C   ('leave the graze uncovered. Exposure to the air ...')
    3   B   ('Bleeding can ... be stopped by applying pressure')
    4   A   (by avoiding long exposure and covering exposed areas)
    5   B   (The limb should be raised. Lying in bed is the easiest way to do this.)

Vocabulary included in the Language review: bite (Insect Bites), relieve (Burns and Scalds)

▶ Focus on grammar 3 Expressing number (p. 175)

Exercise 1

    a   both   f   Neither
    b   Every   g   either
    c   none   h   all
    d   each   i   neither
    e   all   j   either, Both

▶ Focus on writing 2 Report (p. 177)

This would be a suitable writing task for homework or for timed exam practice.

Remind students of the importance of thinking about the intended *reader* and the *purpose* and of including *all* the points mentioned. You may also find it useful to revise key features of reports from the Writing Bank (page 126) beforehand.

▶ Language review (p. 177)

    1   C (Lead-in, 1.3)   9   B (1,2)
    2   A (1,1)   10   D (Lead-in, 1.6)
    3   A (Lead-in, 1.2)   11   C (1,6)
    4   B (1,4)   12   D (Lead-in, 1.6; Study Box 1)
    5   D (1,4)   13   B (Study Box 2)
    6   C (2)   14   C (Focus on grammar 1)
    7   A (1,3)   15   D (Focus on grammar 1)
    8   B (2)

▶ Odd man out (p. 178)

For general notes on this type of exercise see Unit 7, page 28.

    1   *thumb* – the others are parts of the face.
    2   *ribbon* – not used for medical purposes.
    3   *stomach* – the others are joints.
    4   *spot* – the others are injuries.
    5   *eggs* – the others are products made from milk (dairy products).
    6   *boil* – the only method of cooking which uses water.
    7   *chips* – the others are uncountable.
        or *meat* – the only animal product.
    8   *ironmonger's* – the others are food shops.
    9   *judo* – not a ball game.
   10   *Sydney* – the others have held Olympic Games.

UNIT 10 ▶ Narrow escapes

▶ Lead-in (p. 179)

2 1 i, e
   2 c, d, h
   3 a, f
   4 b, g
   Ask students to explain which order the extracts should come in and which words helped them to match the extracts to the headlines.

3 Get students to explain the four narrow escapes to each other and/or the whole class. Let them re-read the extracts, encouraging them to guess any unknown vocabulary, for example, (a) an electrical appliance, to be mystified, dressing table.

Note: The Language check exercise on page 181 includes a number of prepositional phrases from these extracts.

4 Example answers
Although the child fell from a moving car on to the road, he was completely unhurt. It was as if he had been made of rubber and bounced like a ball.

The family have experienced two major accidents in their home in a short period of time. It seems that they are unusually unlucky.

Vocabulary included in the Language review: a second major accident in three months (c), otherwise (e), cause something to happen (f).

▶ Text 1 Crew saves pilot (p. 180)

1 Example answers
   1 The pilot was pulled through the window on to the nose of the plane.
   2 A window came out/broke.
   3 They held on to the pilot's legs to stop him being pulled out completely.

2 As with all gapped text questions, encourage students to look for clues to help them decide which paragraph goes where. Point out the way 'Captain Lancaster ...' in D is followed by 'British Airways later said that *he*', 'The pilot ...' in A is followed by '*His* body ...' It's also worth pointing out how people are usually referred to by their full name first, (e.g. Tim Lancaster and Alistair Aitcheson) and later by a shorter version (e.g. Captain Lancaster and Mr Aitcheson).

   1 D   4 C
   2 B   5 A
   3 E

3 1 False (He broke some bones and had frostbite)
   2 False (The airline praised them)
   3 True (It had been replaced two days earlier)
   4 True (He had been flying for 21 years)
   5 False (The co-pilot flew the plane)
   6 True (There was no panic)

4 1 crew   6 alertness
   2 cockpit   7 windscreen
   3 fuselage   8 was sucked out
   4 fractures   9 clung
   5 frostbite   10 grabbed

5 1 at (Extract a)   5 into (Extract i)
      for (Extract b)   6 in (Extract i)
   2 on (Extract d)   7 in (Extract i)
      to (Extract h)   8 for (Text 1, section 5)
   3 in (Extract c)   9 among(st) (Text 1, section 4)
   4 at (Extract b)   10 in (Text 1, section 1)

▶ Focus on grammar 1 Expressing time (p. 182)

Exercise 1

Before	Same time	Later	Sequence
earlier	while	after	next
	all the time	later	then
	as	when	finally

Example answers
   1 during the performance
      while he's having a bath
      lay the table, please?
   2 first studied all the brochures.
      It was cloudy at first
   3 when spring came at last
   4 we went to a Chinese restaurant
      we went out for a meal

Exercise 2
   1 at first   7 then/next
   2 after   8 finally
   3 during   9 afterwards
   4 while   10 meanwhile
   5 before   11 at last
   6 first(ly)

Exercise 3 (Example answers)
   a gets/arrives   e reach/have reached
   b come to live in   f I'm driving to
   c I've obtained a   g take the examination
   d he's on/he's caught the   h see/have seen

▶ Focus on listening 1 A survival kit (p. 184)

Check that students know the names for the various objects illustrated. Check their understanding of *survival kit* and ask them when such a thing would be useful.

1 a matchbox
   b nylon
   c fishing hook
   d carry water
   e there are no holes in it.
   f candle
   g stretch it too much
   h fish
   i waterproof
   j to write messages
   k whistle

2 9

3 11

Vocabulary included in the Language review: so as to (see also Study Box 2).

▶ Focus on writing 1 Instructions (p. 184)

1
   5
   2
   7
   4
   1
   6
   3

2

3 Place the head of a match in the wax and turn it carefully in order to *cover it completely*.

7 Lay the matches end to end so that *no two matches can touch*.

3 Example answer

Be careful not to get hot wax on your fingers (after 2). Make sure you have sealed them completely (after 6). Once you have done that, (to link any two sentences).

4 Example answer

Making matches waterproof

First, light a candle. Next, hold the candle over the base of the match box and let some wax drip into the base. Be careful not to get any hot wax on your fingers while you're doing this. Then place the head of a match in the wax and turn it carefully in order to cover it completely. Once you've done that, lay the match in the wax and drip wax along the length of the match. Then repeat the process for each match, making sure that they are completely sealed. Lay the matches end to end so that no two heads can touch.

5 Read through the short introduction on the fact sheet and make sure students understand what a solar still is, and what it does.

Check the details on the diagram and encourage students to use purpose clauses from the Study Box below. For example:

Why does the stone have to be smooth?
So that it doesn't tear the plastic sheet.

Check relevant items from the Functions Bank for expressing location. For example:

Where are the stones placed?
On either side of the hole.

Where is the smooth stone placed?
In the middle of the plastic sheet, *over* the container.

Example answer

First you need to choose a suitable place for your solar still. This should be in a low area and in full sunlight, otherwise it will not work. Then use your digging tool to make a hole in the ground which is about one metre deep and one metre across. After that, place a container such as a pan at the bottom in order to collect the water. Next, stretch the plastic sheet across the top of the hole and use some heavy stones to weight it down on either side. Finally, choose a smooth stone and place it in the centre of the plastic sheet so that the sheet hangs down over the container. When you have done that, your solar still is now finished and you only have to wait for the results.

The sun will heat the air in the hole, and water will condense on the underside of the plastic sheet. Drops of water will form and will run down and fall into the container.

▶ Text 2 Rescue from the rapids (p. 186)

1 Example answers

1 Because he was carried away by the strong current and could have been drowned or smashed against the rocks.

2 Leon.

3 He was in a very bad state, unable to breathe properly and shaking.

2 1 D (*he lost his footing*)

2 A (*snatching his left hand in my right*)

3 C (*impossibly trying to grip ... a smooth and shiny rock*)

4 C (*launched himself ... into the centre of the whirlpool*)

5 B

Vocabulary included in the Language review: let go of (line 5), slippery (line 19), a current (line 37).

▶ Communication activity 1 (p. 187)

Allow students to read through the text and explain any vocabulary that is unknown. It is also worth pointing out that foxes don't eat grain!

Tell students to work in pairs or small groups and to rearrange furniture as necessary.

Monitor their work but don't worry if they are not making great use of sequence markers at this stage.

If one student works out the answer quickly, make sure s/he explains it clearly to his/her partner or the rest of the group.

Ask students to take it in turns to explain the answer, one step at a time. Insist that they include sequence markers in their explanation now.

The answer is as follows:

First the man rows to dry land with the chicken, and returns. **Next** he rows across with the fox, and returns with the chicken to the house. **After that** he takes the grain to dry land and returns. **Finally**, he rows across with the chicken.

▶ Focus on grammar 2 Modal verbs 4: Certainty/probability/possibility (p. 188)

Let students discuss their ideas about the picture in pairs first. The chances are that they won't use modal verbs to do this!

When you ask them to report back their ideas, draw their attention to the tables below and ask them to use that language. They should also be encouraged to disagree, using the negative: 'Not, it can't be an African hut' etc.

The 'answer' is shown on page 226, but you may prefer to delay revealing this till later in the lesson.

Practice

This exercise can be extended if students can suggest other examples of their own.

Exercise 1

a My mother may (might/could) have phoned while we were out.

b Helen might (may) have seen the film on TV last night.

c You must have eaten too much at lunch.

d I can't have woken the baby, ...

e John could (might/may) have forgotten the appointment.

f A pipe must have burst while we were away.

g The cleaning lady might (could/may) have thrown your cheque book away by mistake.

▶ Focus on listening 2 (p. 190)

Give students time to read through the questions and to look at the map. Check particularly that they understand the items in the key to the map.

Multiple choice

1	C	5	A
2	C	6	B
3	D	7	D
4	B		

8

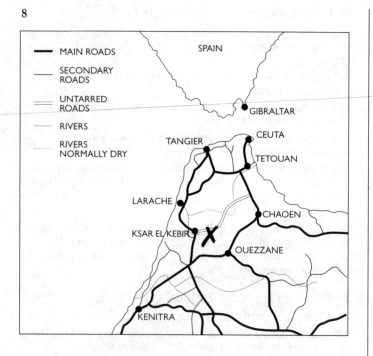

▶ Communication activity 2 Brain-teasers (p. 191)

This activity is designed to provide freer practice in the use of the modal verbs which were presented in the previous grammar section. No introduction is needed, but students should be organised in pairs or small groups as necessary.

Monitor students' work and be prepared to help with any questions about vocabulary. Encourage them to use modal verbs for probability, but do this as unobtrusively as possible.

Afterwards, ask students who are confident that they have discovered the answers to explain them to the rest of the class. Deal with any language problems which arose.

A The car had gone into a river (or lake) and sunk to the bottom. The man had managed to escape by opening the window and then the car door, and swimming to the surface.

B He touched him, because he was in the boat with Dan.

C One train went through the tunnel at 2 p.m. and the other went through at 3 p.m.

D He saw him. It was daylight.

▶ Focus on grammar 3 Question tags (p. 192)

Note: It is useful to do this section immediately, or fairly soon, after Focus on listening 2.

Exercise 1

a	6	f	4
b	5	g	10
c	9	h	1
d	7	i	3
e	2	j	8

Special points

It may also be worth mentioning the special use of question tags where an affirmative tag follows an affirmative statement, or a negative one follows a negative statement. For example:

So you *refuse* to give me my money back, *do you?*
You *won't tell* me where you've been, *won't you?*

These patterns usually imply a particular emotion or attitude. They are often ironic or threatening in tone.

Exercise 2

a	didn't we?	f	should you?
b	have you?	g	didn't we?
c	wouldn't you?	h	did they?
d	will you?	i	will you?
e	aren't there?	j	aren't I?

Notes on pronunciation

You can change the meaning of a question tag by the way you say it. If your voice **falls** at the end of the question tag, you expect your listener to agree with you. It's not a real question. For example:

We've worked hard today, haven't we?

If your voice **rises** at the end, you sound questioning and you expect an answer (either 'yes' or 'no') from your listener. It **is** a real question. For example:

It's not time to go already, is it?

Practise saying the following sentences with both falling and rising intonation:

You can drive, can't you?
Your parents aren't coming, are they?
It's not 6 o'clock yet, is it?
She speaks Russian, doesn't she?
I don't have to pay, do I?

▶ Focus on writing 2 Narrative (p. 194)

Note: This would be a suitable topic for a timed exam practice if you feel students would benefit from the experience of writing in a limited time at this stage of their course.

Read through the notes on the plan and on tenses. Check that students can say **why** the different tenses are used in the examples. In particular, revise the use of the past perfect to express the earlier of two actions in the past (examples 2, 3 and 4).

Find out how many students have had a personal 'narrow escape' that they can write about. Suggest that those who haven't should use the picture at the bottom of the page as the basis for an imaginary account.

If there are a number of students who will be writing an account based on the picture, it would be useful to give them time to work in a group (or groups) to discuss their ideas.

Make sure that all students make a brief plan before they start writing the composition.

▶ Language review (p. 195)

1 D (Focus on grammar 1)
2 C (1C; 2.5)
3 C 2.37

4 B (Focus on grammar 2)
5 B 2.19
6 D (Focus on grammar 3)
7 C (Lead-in 2c)
8 A (Lead-in 2e)

9 C (Lead-in 2f)
10 D (Focus on grammar 2)
11 B (Study Box 2, Focus on listening 1)
12 A (Study Box 2)
13 B (Study Box 2)
14 D (Focus on grammar 1)
15 A (Study Box 3)

UNIT 11 ▶ The market place

▶ **Lead-in Topic vocabulary (p. 196)**

The photographs can be used to provide practice for Paper 5 (Speaking) in the examination.

Possible approaches

a Write a number of questions on the board. Students discuss the answers in pairs or small groups.

Example questions

What is for sale here?
Would you find places like these in your country? Is so, where?
What differences would there be in buying things in these two places?
Which place attracts you most? Why?
What would be the advantages and disadvantages of shopping in these two places?

b Students take it in turns to ask and answer questions about the picture.

c Students follow the 'Witness' procedure (see page 18).

d Perhaps initiate a brief discussion of different methods of buying and selling.

1
1	a butcher	5	a newsagent
2	a baker	6	a tobacconist
3	a fishmonger	7	a chemist/pharmacist
4	a greengrocer	8	a grocer

2
1	the box office	5	a travel agent's (agency)
2	the booking office	6	a stationer's
3	a bookshop	7	an estate agent's
4	a petrol station/filling station service station/garage	8	an ironmonger's

3
1	a hairdresser's (barber's)	3	a laundry
2	a shoemender's/cobbler's	4	a laundrette

4
a slice (cold meat*)
b bar (soap, chocolate)
c bunch (flowers, grapes)
d roll (bandage, wallpaper)
e pair (gloves)
* although actually sold in slices, the cost is by weight

▶ **Text 1 Down the aisle (p. 197)**

1 You could cover the discussion points which follow the text here if you prefer.

Remind students that it is important to read the text quickly for general understanding before beginning the matching task.

0	E (example)	4	D
1	C	5	B
2	A	6	F
3	H		

Vocabulary included in the Language review: depend on (section 2), a display (section 3), attract (someone's) attention (section 3).

▶ **Focus on grammar 1 The passive voice (p. 198)**

Examples from text

You're very easily *persuaded*
decisions ... *are made* suddenly
... a product is *displayed* ...
You *are faced with* ...
products ... *are placed*
When the film *is speeded up*

Exercise 1 (Example answers)

Tense	Subject	Verb *to be*	Past participle
Present simple	Dinner	..........is........	served
Present continuous	A new hospital	is being	built
Present Perfect	A stolen car	has been	found
Past simple	The thief	was	....arrested......
Past continuous	The room	....was being...	painted
Past Perfect	The decision	had been	taken
Future simple	Your offer	will be	...considered.....
Future perfect	*The invitations.*	will have been	posted
OTHER STRUCTURES			
Going to	His car	...is going to be...	serviced
Modals (Present)	This machine	can ....be.........	mended
(Past)	.....This letter.....	shouldn't have been	opened

Exercise 2

1	g	5	f
2	c	6	b
3	h	7	d
4	a	8	e

Exercise 3 (Example answers)

a Dogs must/should be kept on a lead/under control.
b Cheques cannot be accepted./Payment cannot be made by cheque.
c Smoking is not allowed/permitted.
d Shoes must be removed (before entering the mosque).
e Cigarettes must/should be placed in the ashtrays.
f Helmets must/are to be worn on this site.

In each case, ask where the sign might be seen.

Exercise 4

a is cut down
b be built
c are spent
d also be saved; were made
e be ground up, mixed...and sold
f has only been beaten
g was probably painted
h was being washed
i is being written
j are still denied
k will not be forgotten
l have been delayed
m was spilt
n Will the votes be/have been counted
o had been broken into

▶ **Focus on listening 1 Chips with everything (p. 200)**

System	Town	Equipment needed	Home delivery?	Cost
Over-60s Shopping Line	Gateshead	☎ ✓ / ▣ ✓ / ? ☐	✓	free
Club 403	Birmingham	☎ ✓ / ▣ ✓ / ? ☐	✓	£6.50 every 3 months
Shopping Link	South London	☎ ✓ / ▣ ☐ / ? ☐	✓	£1.73 for each order
Comp-ú-Card	Windsor	☎ ☐ / ▣ ☐ / ? ✓	✓	£20 to join

Vocabulary included in the Language review: stock

▶ Text 2 Buying by post (p. 200)

2 2   check that the newspaper ... is up to date. (1)
    3   keep details of the advertisement ... advertiser's address ...(5)
    6,7 When you write off (and ... return goods) always include your name and address. (3)
    8   Make sure you keep cheque stubs or counterfoils. (7)
    9   Keep a ... note of the date it was sent. (4)

3 1   B (*fit in seconds*)
    2   D (*Order now while stocks last.*)
    3   A (*without pulling or stretching their delicate fibres*)
    4   B (*Do not confuse with inferior models.*)
    5   D (*your worries are over.*)
    6,7 A,C (*No home should be without one'*, '*Indispensable/A must in any first-aid box.*)

Vocabulary included in the Language review: to write off (for), a receipt, proof, to stretch, relief, protect from, stock(s).

▶ Focus on writing Part 1 Formal letter (p. 202)

Preparation

1 Revise details of formal letter writing:

Layout – sender's and recipient's addresses; date; beginning and ending (see Writing Bank p. 114).

Style – neither too formal nor too colloquial (see note on p. 143).

2 If you feel your students still need help with this type of writing, work with the class to draw up a suitable plan on the board.

First paragraph	Explain exactly why you are writing.
Middle paragraph(s)	Give full details (see list under 'If you have to complain')
Last paragraph	Explain what you would like the recipient to do.

Alternatively, you could set this task for homework or as timed exam practice.

▶ Focus on listening 2 The auctioneer (p. 202)

Note: Before students open their books, introduce the topic by drawing an auctioneer's hammer on the board and asking what it is and where they would see it used. If the class needs more help, tell them it is associated with a particular kind of buying and selling.

Even if students don't know the term 'auction', ask them to describe how an auction works. Introduce the topic vocabulary from page 202 and ask if anyone has ever attended an auction.

How do you show that you want to bid? (Be careful not to give a definite right answer here.) What are the advantages and disadvantages? Are there any dangers?

1 1 C (*an opportunity came up to move into the auction side of the business*)
    2 D (*it's normally raising the catalogue*)
    3 C (*it's often a bit of a joke; a bit of light relief*)
    4 A (*getting slightly carried away*)

2 5 False. (*a lot of people ... want to go and have a look around the house as well as the contents*)
    6 True. (*in an appalling condition – you could hardly see what was actually underneath it*)
    7 False. (*we were hoping it would get something around there*)
    8 True.
    9 False. (*I'm called upon to value items in a very broad sense ...*)
    10 furniture/wood
    11 can't afford
    12 scared

▶ Communication activity Selling pets (p. 204)

Preparation

You may prefer to elicit selected items of functional language, put these on the board, and then practise for appropriate stress and intonation.

Decide which students should work together in pairs and ask them to read their instructions.

Find a way of telling A students which animal they have to sell without their partner hearing. The element of surprise created will help to make the role play more lively and realistic. You could either whisper the name of the animal or write it on slips of paper.

Once A students have told their partners which role to take, the role play should start.

Role play

Monitor the conversations but avoid offering advice or interrupting unless absolutely necessary. Note what language is used and what expressions are not included. Note, too, any particular errors.

After 5 minutes, tell students to change roles. Give B students the name of another animal in the way described above.

Feedback

Ask for brief responses from students to the discussion points. Deal with any language problems that you noted.

Note: Unless any pair particularly wants to perform their conversation in front of the class at this point, it is probably not a good idea to suggest it. The second-time-round conversations are likely to be more self-conscious and less spontaneous.

▶ Text 3 (p. 205)

2 1   C
    2   C (*You are likely to spend less if you leave the children behind.*)
    3   A (*Try to plan your cooking to have a full oven.*)
    4   B (*Think particularly carefully about running a second car.*)
    5   D (*Buying food in large packets and bulk quantities.*)

Vocabulary included in the Language review: to get by (C), take advantage of (A)

▶ Focus on grammar 2 Gerund and infinitive (p. 206)

Exercise 1

a   to call; to order
b   typing; to concentrate
c   to telephone; servicing
d   to make; raining
e   buying; painting; decorating
f   to say; promising
g   taking; to buy
h   to try; shouting

Exercise 2

a   asking; to raise; to do
b   to stop; working; to call
c   thinking; to lend
d   using; to borrow; typing
e   taking; not to call
f   to hear; to visit; seeing

▶ Language review (p. 208)

1	A (3 C; Unit 4 Study Box 2)	9	C (2)
2	D (2)	10	C (2, Listening 1)
3	B (2, Question 3.1)	11	A (2)
4	D (1, 3)	12	D (3 A)
5	C (1, 3)	13	D (2)
6	B (2)	14	A (Study Box 2)
7	C (1, 2)	15	B (Focus on grammar 2)
8	B (2)		

UNIT 12 ▶ Turning points

▶ ## Lead-in 1 (p. 209)

Note: It is best if students work in pairs or small groups initially for this activity.

1   Ask students to decide what is happening (or has happened) in each picture, and to give reasons for their opinions, using information in the pictures. For example, 'In picture D, I think the couple have just got married because the woman is wearing a white dress and head-dress, and is holding a bouquet of flowers.'

Remind students to use language which shows a range of probability. For example:

	may	
(I think) it/he/ she/they	could must	be/have been
he/she seems	+ adjective + to + infinitive	

Ask students to discuss the second part of question 1. For example:

A (first day at school): becoming more independent, making friends, developing interests in particular subjects which might lead to a career, etc.

2   Again ask students to discuss this question in pairs/groups and to try to reach agreement. They should be prepared to explain their reasons to the class afterwards.

3, 4   These questions can be discussed by the class as a whole, unless numbers make this difficult.

▶ ## Lead-in 2 (p. 210)

Give students time to read through the extracts fairly quickly (2–3 minutes) and then ask them to discuss their ideas with another student.

Establish that they all refer to the experience of winning a large sum of money, and ask how this could have happened (football pools, lottery, etc.).

2   1   A   (possibly C)
2   C
3   They probably didn't feel that s/he was the same as them any more. They may have felt that it was strange to buy drinks for someone who was so much richer than they were, yet they didn't want him/her to pay for everything either.
4   He must have thought that he should have received some money, or else that his £800 wasn't a generous enough gift for his son.
5   Begging letters were letters from people asking for money. Proposals could have been offers of marriage, or perhaps offers concerning business matters. The winner's new friends must be people who are interested in her because of her new wealth. She's fed up with them because they aren't real friends, and they seem to be rather a nuisance.
6   A person might become proud/arrogant/snobbish. They might reject their old friends or show off to them by spending money in large amounts.

7   It depends on the friendship. I don't think it would affect a really old friendship which had lasted a number of years, but with newer friends, it could be difficult because suddenly my friend would be able to buy expensive things and take expensive holidays. The only way I could share my friend's new lifestyle would be if s/he paid for me, and that wouldn't be comfortable for either of us.

Vocabulary included in the Language review: to react (B), to give up (D) (see also Study Box 1).

▶ ## Focus on grammar 1
Expressing wishes and regrets (p. 210)

Exercise 1 (Example answers)

I wish/If only ...
a   it wasn't raining.
b   I could drive./I knew how to drive.
c   I didn't have such an awful headache./the party wasn't this evening.
d   he/she didn't snore so loudly./I could get to sleep.
e   there was/were more time.
f   I had a map./knew the way.

Exercise 2 (Example answers)

I wish/If only ...
a   I hadn't been going so fast./I had had the brakes repaired.
b   I had listened to the weather forecast./it hadn't started raining.
c   I hadn't forgotten the cake./I had read the recipe more carefully.
d   I hadn't been caught./I had kept away from crime.
e   I had read the notice./I hadn't decided to sit down.
f   I hadn't tried to cross this field./I had seen the bull in time.

Exercise 3 (Example answers)

a   It's high time you cleaned it./had it cleaned!
b   Suppose you had an accident./you had your luggage stolen.
c   Why do you still treat me as if I were a child?
d   She'd rather you took her fruit.

▶ ## Text 1 Just a normal day? (p. 212)

1 Suggested answers

1   She won it in a newspaper competition.
2   She suspected that she might have won on Saturday morning when she checked her competition card, but she was quite sure by 6 o'clock that evening.
3   She's afraid she won't be able to continue going to bingo with her friends.

2   1   C
2   B (*to save on electricity*)
3   A (*You can't take it in, can you?*)
4   C
5   D (*all my friends*)

Discussion points B

1   1   I would probably feel better if I took more exercise.
2   If she didn't have a dog for company, she'd be quite lonely.
3   If you won £1,000, how would you spend the money?

5   After students have decided individually on their answers to the three questions, monitor the pairwork. Note when and how accurately the second conditional is used and what reasons are given.

Ask pairs to report back. This will be more effective if students are asked to report back on what their **partner** said.

The sequel

Allow students to read these short texts silently and to comment on how accurate their predictions were (Discussion points A). Check comprehension as necessary.

Vocabulary included in the Language review: take something in (see also Study Box 2).

▶ Focus on writing 1 Exam practice (p. 214)

The two Focus on writing sections in this unit provide practice in each of the main types of writing required in the examination: letters, articles, reports and compositions. It is a good opportunity to review the main features of language, style and organisation in each case. In particular stress the importance of planning the structure and content in note form in advance. Lack of pre-planning is one of the most common reasons for poor work in the Writing paper of the examination.

In general, it's a good idea to involve students in discussing how to tackle the various topics beforehand. Working in groups, they can read through the notes and refer to the Writing Bank before a whole-class summarising session. The final writing, however, should be done individually, and preferably within a time limit of 45 minutes per topic.

If students are taking the *First Certificate* examination shortly, a timed practice session would be extremely useful. This should take 1 1/2 hours and be under examination conditions (no discussion, no reference to the course book or dictionaries). Students should write the Part 1 formal letter and select one other topic from Focus on writing 1 and 2, to be completed in the time.

1 Formal Letter (Part 1)

Remind students that in this section it is vital to read the instructions and any other information *very carefully*. If they don't do exactly what is asked or if they don't cover every point, they will lose marks.

2 Report

A useful preparation phase would be a 'brainstorming' session in groups of 3 – 5. Give students about 5 – 10 minutes to make a Top 10 list of tourist attractions in the town where you are. This will help stimulate ideas and provide practice in justifying choices.

▶ Focus on listening 1 Is there life after redundancy? (p. 215)

1 Check the difference between 'to be made redundant' and 'to be dismissed' or 'to be sacked'.

2 Give students time to study the table before playing the tape.

	Previous career	Length of time (years)	Redundancy pay	New career	Where?	Success? Yes/No/ Too early to say
A Brian Collins	1. Electrical industry 2. Teaching sailing	a. 4	b. £350	c. boat repair firm	Scotland	yes
B William Rudd	Chemical company	d. 20	£70,000	e. butcher's shop	f. central London	g. yes
C Patricia and Rex Pole	h. bank	33	i. £30,000	j. running a pub	South Coast	k. no
D Graham Clarke	l. Salesman	m. 27	n. £2,000	magician	Colchester	o. too early to say

Vocabulary included in the Language review : in recent years

▶ Communication activity Turning points in history (p. 216)

Note: Since few students are likely to know more than one or two answers for certain, it may be necessary to re-emphasise that they should guess those they don't know, and that they must choose an answer for each question.

1 Monitor students' discussions and be prepared to help with any vocabulary problems.

Check students' answers in a class discussion before they look up the answers on page 226. Ask those who are confident of an answer to give reasons.

2 Pairs could award themselves marks for correct answers so that there will be a winning pair in the general knowledge quiz.

3 For variety of interaction, ask pairs to form groups of four in order to discuss these two questions. Emphasise that they must agree on one answer in each case, and that they must be prepared to give their reasons. Ask groups to report back afterwards.

4 Again, this will be more effective, and involve more communication, if groups first 'brainstorm' their ideas. Each group can then make one or two suggestions for the class to consider.

Vocabulary included in the Language review: take place.

▶ Focus on grammar 2 Conditional 3 (p. 217)

Exercise 1

a If Mrs Barrett hadn't bought the *Daily Mirror*, she wouldn't have taken part in the competition.

b If she had forgotten to check the numbers on her card, she wouldn't have won a million pounds.

c She wouldn't have rung her daughter if she hadn't been so excited.

d If Annie hadn't been so tired, she wouldn't have gone back to sleep.

e She wouldn't have been interviewed if she hadn't become a millionairess.

f (Example answer) If she hadn't won so much money, she couldn't have moved from her council flat or bought a new television.

Exercise 2

a If the Incas had had paper, their architects wouldn't have needed to make clay models for the builders to follow./their architects could have drawn plans for the builders to follow.

b If Napoleon hadn't died in 1821, he might have had his photograph taken./If the camera had been invented earlier, Napoleon might have been photographed.

c Many lives would have been lost during World War II if penicillin hadn't been invented.

d Christopher Columbus might not have reached the West Indies in 1492 if the mariner's compass hadn't been invented.

e (Example answer) If tobacco hadn't been imported to Europe in 1553, the habit of smoking might never have developed.

Mixed Conditionals

Exercise

a If the Suez Canal hadn't been opened in 1869, ships would have to travel round Africa to reach India.

b If the Panama Canal hadn't been completed in 1914, ships would have to sail round South America to reach the Pacific.

c Ships would have to go round the Peloponnese to reach the Aegean Sea if the Corinth Canal hadn't been built in 1893.

Optional extra practice

Work with a partner. Think what life would be like today if the things below had never been invented. Discuss how your lives would be different.

    a   Clock (1290)
    b   Wheel (4,000 BC)
    c   Telephone (1876)
    d   Television (1926)

▶ Text 2 Love in a strange climate (p. 218)

Begin with a brief discussion of wedding conventions in the students' countries as compared with British traditions. You could consider such questions as: who pays for the wedding; what is thrown over the bride and groom; what it means if you catch the wedding bouquet; and what is tied to the car of the newly-weds as they leave. You could also teach/revise topic vocabulary like *bride, groom, best man, bridesmaid*, etc. (Note: *honeymoon* is checked in Exercise 2, and *marriage v wedding* are dealt with in Exercise 4.)

2	1	B		7, 8	B, F
	2	C		9	A
	3	A		10	D
	4	F		11	F
	5, 6	E, G		12	A

3	1	congregation		5	honeymoon
	2	strolled		6	economics
	3	pastor		7	significant
	4	brief			

6					
	1	wedding		5	wedding
	2	marriage		6	has been married to
	3	get married		7	marriage
	4	marriages		8	wedding

Vocabulary included in the Language review: despite (paragraph 5), ahead of (time) (6).

▶ Focus on grammar 3 Review of tenses (p. 221)

Exercise 1

    a   I'll give; he comes in.
    b   He ran; he got; the bus had already gone.
    c   I wouldn't offer; I thought; wouldn't pay.
    d   You've broken; you'll have to
    e   does this train get
    f   It says; paintings have been stolen.
    g   I told; I wanted; I had found.
    h   you don't/won't stop; I'll call.
    i   We're going; it will be; we usually tour
    j   you haven't been waiting; the lift has broken down; I had to.
    k   we were waiting; the pilot announced; we were going to fly/would be flying.
    l   I've been working; this page is finished; I'll have written.
    m   We bought; we needn't have done so.
    n   I hadn't seen; I would never have believed.
    o   you didn't smoke; you don't mind; smoke always makes.

Exercise 1

    A   I haven't seen; have you been doing?
    B   I've been working; I had; I only got.
    A   were you living?
    B   I spent; I went.
    A   did you manage
    B   I climbed; I also saw; it is called.
    A   did you take
    B   didn't come out; I was using; didn't have; I had taken
    A   you'll show; I had known you were going; I would have asked.
    B   I was invited; I didn't have
    A   I was only joking; are you doing
    B   My parents are coming; they will leave/will have left.
    A   don't you come; you'll be able to
    B   I'll even bring

Exercise 3

Paragraph 1	Paragraph 2
left	decided
found	to take
to get	to earn
must have written	to pay
said	was serving
to tell	talking
applied	explained/was explaining
has now been filled	had left/was leaving
had	didn't know
told	to do
had been	stopped
didn't get	serving
	asked
	would consider
	had
	must have been
	agreed
	to interview
	was given
	have been working
	would still be serving
	hadn't had

▶ Focus on listening 2 A new direction (p. 222)

Find out if students remember the conversation with John, the merchant seaman, from Unit 2. For example, ask questions like:

    How long did he work in the Merchant Navy?
    Did he enjoy the life?
    Why did he leave?

Point out that the conversation they are going to hear is with the same man, and in it he discusses the complete change of career which occurred after he left the Merchant Navy.

True/false

  1 False. (*I remembered seeing the nurses work in hospital and I thought "I'd quite like to do that"*)
  2 False. (*I could've worked in a hotel ...*)
  3 True. (*... provided you have the right educational qualifications*)
  4 False. (*I started where I finished ... I never left it.*)
  5 True. (*... 3 years' training initially and then ... 2 years' training in mental illness*)
  6 False. (*There's really no difference.*)
  7 True.
  8 True. (*The pay was very low compared with the Merchant Navy*)
  9 True. (Most were in their teens. He was 31.)
 10 False. (*I didn't want to be living in the nurses' home ...*)
 11 B (*Moving from ward to ward*)
 12 C (*I wanted to go on learning ... it was the next logical step.*)
 13 D (*No regrets whatsoever. Even the bad things I don't regret.*)

▶ Focus on writing 2 Exam practice (p. 223)

For general notes about the writing tasks in this unit, see Focus on writing 1 (page 40). For each task, remind students to think carefully about the purpose of writing, the reader, and the layout and style for the particular kind of writing.

1 Informal Letter

The main points to revise here are the layout of an informal letter and aspects of language and style. (See Writing Bank page 112) A good way of revising these would be to produce a 'bad' letter which includes examples of all the common mistakes (see Student's Book page 37 for ideas) and ask students to identify the faults. Alternatively, elicit the main points from the students.

Stress the importance of achieving the main aim – to make the reader understand and accept the situation despite any disappointment or annoyance they might feel.

2 Narrative

Revise expressions of time and the use of past tenses, as indicated. Refer students to the paragraph plan on page 194 and the Writing Bank pages 122-3.

Remind students that they will probably find it easier to write about a real event but that they can add details or invent a story if necessary.

3 Discussion

Students need to consider both the structure and language of a discussion and the approach of an article and they should study the relevant information in the Writing Bank beforehand.

One way of revising language points would be to prepare a gap-fill exercise based on a discussion topic, where key phrases and link words are missing.

▶ Language review (p. 224)

1	C (Lead-in 2B)	9	D (2 para 5)
2	B (1.71; Study Box 2)	10	B (Unit 11 Study Box 2)
3	D (Communic. Activity)	11	C (Unit 9 Study Box 1)
4	C (Focus on grammar 2)	12	D (Focus on grammar 1)
5	A (Listening 1)	13	B (Writing 2)
6	D (Functions Bank)	14	A (Unit 9 Study Box 1)
7	C (Lead-in 2D; Study Box 1)	15	B (Functions Bank)
8	A (2 para 6)		

EXAM PRACTICE Use of English

This section contains five complete Use of English tests. Teachers can either set individual tasks for extra practice as the course progresses or reserve the tests for more intensive exam preparation towards the end of the course. Students should be allowed 1 hour 15 minutes to complete a 'mock' test.

The five parts of the test are as follows

Part 1 Multiple choice cloze

A text with 15 gaps and multiple choice answers to choose from. The main focus here is on vocabulary.

- Encourage students to read the whole text through quickly before they start choosing answers so they have a general idea of what it's about.

- Answers must fit the meaning *and* grammar of the sentence. In considering the answers, students should look carefully at the prepositions which follow verbs, at verb complementation (e.g. -*ing* or *to* + *infinitive*), and at verbs which precede nouns (e.g. *make* or *do*)

Part 2 Open cloze

A text with 15 gaps in it. The main focus here is on grammar.

- Again, encourage students to read the whole text before they think about possible answers.

- Help them to think about the part of speech which is needed in each gap. Prepositions, auxiliary and modal auxiliary verbs are often needed, as are link words (e.g. *but*, *and*. *although*) and parts of phrasal verbs.

Part 3 'Key' word transformation

10 sentences have to be rewritten using a given word so that the meaning stays the same. This task focuses on grammar and vocabulary, and a very wide range of structures as well as phrasal verbs and common phrases can be tested.

- Make sure that students understand the 'rules': the 'key' word mustn't be changed in any way, and they mustn't write more than five words including the 'key' word.

- Revise all the common structures like verb tenses, conditionals, passives and reported speech, and give students plenty of practice with phrasal verbs and modal verbs as well.

Part 4 Error Correction

A text in which most (but not all) lines contain an extra and unnecessary word. Students must write the extra words in the spaces provided and put a tick next to the correct lines. The focus is on grammar.

- Encourage students to read the whole text first, concentrating on the meaning.

- Advise them to read it again very carefully, line by line. It's easy to miss mistakes when you read too quickly.

- Warn them that while some structures look correct they may not fit with the meaning or grammar of the context. For example, an unnecessary *no* or *not* can give the opposite meaning to that intended.

Part 5 Word formation

A text with 10 gaps in it. A word is provided in each case and this must be changed in some way to fit the gap. The focus is on vocabulary.

Typical changes are verb to noun (e.g. *vary-variety*) noun to adjective (e.g. *skill-skilful*), and noun to adverb (e.g. *care-carefully*) but in addition the word may need to be made plural (e.g. *strong-strengths*) or negative (e.g. *appear-disappearance*) to fit the context.

• Encourage students to think in terms of word families: noun, adjective, verb, adverb and to record and learn vocabulary in this way.

• Give students plenty of practice with prefixes (e.g. *dis-, in-, un-* etc) and suffixes (e.g. *-ment, -ation, -ful, -less* etc)

• Point out places where more than one word can be formed (e.g. *harmful* and *harmless*), and discuss with students which makes better sense in the context.

Answers

TEST 1 ▶

▶ PART 1 Michelle's Story

1	B	9	D
2	D	10	A
3	B	11	D
4	C	12	C
5	A	13	A
6	C	14	D
7	A	15	B
8	B		

▶ PART 2 First read the small print

1	in	9	but
2	in	10	before
3	go	11	As/Since/Because
4	happens	12	been
5	will	13	before/earlier
6	on	14	us/her
7	had	15	sure
8	to		

▶ PART 3

1 keen on playing
2 was such an unexpected reply
3 which/that used to sell
4 is a tool for cutting
5 takes more time than/takes a longer time than
6 the worst driver
7 did my best to
8 looking forward to hearing   from
9 put me through to
10 make room for

▶ PART 4 Young Driver

1	to	9	✓
2	much	10	could
3	✓	11	out
4	about	12	✓
5	✓	13	to
6	the	14	✓
7	been	15	learn (also begin!)
8	(*the second*) as		

▶ PART 5 Exercise

1	weight	6	outlook
2	management	7	tension
3	strengthen	8	powerful
4	lessens	9	happiness
5	increasingly	10	fitness

TEST 2 ▶

▶ PART 1 Home Security

1	C	9	A
2	D	10	D
3	A	11	A
4	D	12	B
5	B	13	D
6	C	14	C
7	B	15	B
8	C		

▶ PART 2: Young Skater

1	between	9	in
2	than	10	By
3	then	11	least
4	It	12	take
5	being	13	wake/get
6	had/took/started	14	only
7	for/about	15	who
8	at/during		

▶ PART 3

1 prevented us from
2 first time she has been
3 hasn't been able to
4 broke down in
5 disapprove of me/my staying
6 needn't have written
7 is big enough for/to take
8 get away with
9 reminded me of
10 could have been

▶ PART 4 Time Off

1	of	9	✓
2	will	10	after
3	✓	11	of
4	the	12	✓
5	up	13	got
6	✓	14	✓
7	as	15	that
8	been		

▶ PART 5 Amelia Earhart

1 unsolved
2 flight
3 appearances
4 invitations
5 height
6 pressure
7 achievements
8 unsuccessful
9 accompanies
10 departure

TEST 3 ▶

▶ PART 1 Robots

1	A	9	C
2	B	10	A
3	B	11	D
4	C	12	B
5	D	13	C
6	A	14	A
7	D	15	D
8	B		

▶ PART 2 Shipwreck

1	up	9	up
2	By	10	can
3	had	11	instance/example
4	least	12	for
5	In	13	less
6	Before	14	spoil/ruin/destroy
7	proportion/amount/part	15	from
8	would		

▶ PART 3

1 in spite of the heavy
2 unless someone mends it
3 as a result of
4 in case I'm not
5 has set in
6 will have started
7 cut down (on) (your)
8 no use phoning
9 once you've switched on
10 he might be able to

▶ PART 4 A year in South America

1	the	9	✓
2	✓	10	all
3	who	11	✓
4	years	12	ago
5	✓	13	for
6	it	14	✓
7	more	15	be
8	had		

▶ PART 5 Preparing for exams

1 revision
2 variety
3 carefully
4 (e)specially
5 strengths
6 additional
7 confidence
8 occasionally
9 irregular
10 helpful

TEST 4 ▶

▶ PART 1 Adventure Travel

1	B	9	D
2	D	10	C
3	A	11	B
4	C	12	D
5	A	13	A
6	C	14	B
7	A	15	D
8	B		

▶ PART 2 Village Life

1	needed	9	hardly/don't
2	for	10	make/take
3	few	11	in
4	in	12	by
5	Unless	13	doing
6	but	14	too
7	away/far	15	by
8	manages/tries		

▶ PART 3

1 difficulty (in) persuading
2 if you would ('d) mind putting
3 would rather travel by train
4 more carefully you work the
5 apologised for keeping/having kept
6 arrived the train had already
7 advised us not to
8 too cold to
9 look the word
10 had better book

▶ PART 4 Weather Forecaster

1	up	9	✓
2	✓	10	are
3	from	11	✓
4	in	12	be
5	✓	13	the
6	about	14	✓
7	long	15	more
8	can		

▶ PART 5 Photographing Sport

1 composition
2 decisions
3 practice
4 skilful
5 patience
6 Professional
7 apply
8 investment
9 physically
10 enable

TEST 5 ▶

▶ PART 1 Minor Illnesses

1	A	9	A
2	B	10	D
3	D	11	B
4	C	12	C
5	B	13	A
6	C	14	D
7	A	15	B
8	D		

▶ PART 2 Balloon Ride

1	sitting	9	able
2	to	10	was
3	with	11	was
4	which/that	12	for
5	As/While	13	soon
6	feel/get	14	will
7	with	15	had
8	had		

▶ PART 3

1 twice as many guests as
2 great deal of money
3 may have hidden
4 steep hills on either side
5 takes after
6 during the flight
7 have gone if I had
8 to know if Sylvia had
9 had my car repaired
10 is going in for

▶ PART 4 Interview

1	as	9	who
2	✓	10	✓
3	were	11	of
4	of	12	✓
5	being	13	much
6	✓	14	could
7	to	15	to
8	✓		

▶ PART 5 Marconi

1	inventor	6	foundation
2	succeeded	7	fame
3	distance	8	connection
4	encouragement	9	historic
5	engineer	10	successfully

EXAM PRACTICE Listening

The eight tasks in this section provide practice for the four different parts of the Listening paper in the *First Certificate* examination:

Part 1 Multiple choice questions based on listening to a series of short unrelated extracts. (Tasks 1 and 5)

Part 2 A note-taking or blank-filling task based on a longer listening text. (Tasks 2 and 6)

Part 3 Multiple matching questions based on a series of short extracts on the same theme. (Tasks 3 and 7)

Part 4 A task involving selection from two or three possible answers, based on a longer listening text. (Tasks 4 and 8)

The tasks can be done in any order. Since these task types may be new for your students, make sure they read the instructions for each one *very* carefully before they start listening. Tell them that each question will be read out on the tape and that each piece will be played twice. They will have time before the first and second hearings to think about their answer(s).

Remind students that in the examination they will have to fill in their answers on an answer sheet.

Notes for PART 1: Each extract is repeated in turn. Students should use the few seconds they are given before and between the two playings to look through the possible answers. It's important to listen for clues about where the speakers are and what they are talking about.

► SITUATIONS 1 (p. 255)

If you want to introduce this type of task gently, you could go through the first five extracts with the students. Play each one twice and then let students compare notes before you check answers. You could then highlight the key words or phrases which lead to the correct answer.

Key
1	B	5	C
2	C	6	A
3	B	7	C
4	A	8	B

Notes for PART 2: Students will have about 45 seconds to look through the questions before they hear the interview and they should use the time to think about the *type* of information which is needed (e.g. a number? a place? a period of time?). Thinking about the answers in advance in this way will help make the listening task easier.

► WILDLIFE ARTIST (p. 256)

Ask what kind of animals wolves are, and where they are found. If you want to give students more help, go through some of the questions (2, 4, 6, 7, 8 and 10, for example) discussing possible answers.

Key
1	6 or 7	6	they licked his hands/him
2	(he) takes photographs	7	(different) pencils
3	(the) detailed work	8	(a) rabbit, (a) goat, (a) fox
4	Portugal	9	his brother
5	2 weeks	10	they have no purpose (at all)

Notes for PART 3: All five extracts are played through and then repeated. Students will have about 30 seconds before the first playing to think about what they have to do and to read through the list of possible answers.

► TRANSPORT (p. 256)

Tasks with one word options like this one are generally easier than those with longer options, so this provides a suitable introduction. If you want to make the task easier still, you could ask students to suggest advantages and disadvantages for each form of transport, and revise some topic vocabulary before they listen.

Key
1	D	4	E
2	F	5	A
3	C		

Notes for PART 4: There are several different possibilities for this task including **true/false, yes/no, multiple choice** and **who said what** questions. Students will have one minute before they hear the listening text and it's important that they use this time to read through the instructions and the questions.

► BUDDY DOGS (p. 256)

It's not necessary to explain the Buddy Dogs scheme in advance but you may like to check the use of *buddy* (originally an American use) to mean 'close friend'. Multiple choice questions like these involve quite a lot of reading and so it's especially important to read through the questions beforehand. Reading the questions in advance also helps by giving you a general picture of the subject.

Key
1	C	5	A
2	B	6	C
3	A	7	B
4	B		

► SITUATIONS 2 (p. 257)

See notes for Part 1 above.

Key
1	B	5	A
2	C	6	C
3	B	7	B
4	A	8	A

► EXTRAS (p. 258)

See notes for Part 2 above.

As a lead-in to the topic, you could ask students why people might want to work as extras and what kind of people film companies might want to employ as extras. You could also ask if they would like to be extras themselves, and which films they would have liked to be an extra in!

Key
1	funny (and) romantic	6	at least thirty pounds (£30) a day
2	between 300 and 550 (300 – 550)	7	two meals a day
3	a really/very tall (gentle) man	8	(a) hotel/(a) disco
4	(some) acting skills	9	four (4) weeks
5	film and television	10	(next) Tuesday evening

► MEMORIES (p. 259)

See notes for Part 3 above.

As an introduction, you could ask students to think about how each of the items on the list A–F has changed compared with the way it was, say, 50 years ago. This discussion should elicit topic vocabulary which will help students as they listen for clues in the extracts later.

Key
1	C	4	F
2	E	5	D
3	A		

► COMPETITION (p. 259)

See notes for Part 4 above.

In this 'Who said what?' type of question, it's very important to understand exactly what you have to do, so check the instructions with students beforehand. Tell them the questions are in the same order as the information on the tape, but the wording in the questions may differ slightly from the wording on the tape so they need to listen particularly carefully.

As a way of revising topic vocabulary, you could begin by asking what things waiters and waitresses might be tested on in the competition.

Key	1	P		5	J
	2	C		6	C
	3	P		7	P
	4	J			

EXAM PRACTICE Speaking

In the Speaking paper of the *First Certificate* examination there are two candidates and two examiners. One of the examiners asks questions and guides the discussion while the other watches and assesses.

The Speaking paper is in four parts:

Part 1 The candidates talk to the examiner and give information about themselves. (4 minutes)

Part 2 Each candidate talks about two photographs for a minute. (4 minutes)

Part 3 The candidates work together to carry out a communication activity. (3 minutes)

Part 4 The candidates and examiner discuss further questions related to the theme of Part 3. (4 mins)

This section provides practice for Parts 2, 3 and 4. The activities can be used individually at any stage of the course or they can be reserved for more intensive practice or 'mock' interviews as the exam approaches.

▶ PART 1

This is the introductory phase of the interview where the examiner puts the candidates at their ease by asking general conversation questions like: *Where are you from? Have you got any special hobbies?*

Practice activities

Students should be used to answering this kind of question as a routine part of their course. You can give them extra focused practice nearer the time of the exam. Here are some example questions:

Why are you learning English?
What are your plans for the future?
What sport do you like to watch/play?
How do you like to spend your free time?
What programmes do you watch on TV?
What kind of music do you like?
How much exercise do you take?
How do you like living in ...?
Tell me about your family.
What's your favourite food?

▶ PART 2

The pictures usually provide some opportunity for describing and comparing but you should discourage students from giving very detailed, plodding descriptions.

Point out that the pictures should also serve as jumping off points for expressing their personal opinions and preferences. In other words, the examiner will want to hear not only an appropriate description of the pictures (or the situation represented by the pictures) but also a reaction to what's shown.

For this reason it would be very useful to revise relevant language for giving **opinions** (see Functions Bank page 105), expressing **likes, dislikes** and **preferences** (see Functions Bank page 105), and for **speculating** (see Student's Book page 189).

Practice activities

Occasionally ask students to work in pairs or groups to study a picture and then to pool ideas and vocabulary for talking about it. Useful language can be collated on the board afterwards. Nearer the time of the exam it would be helpful to have class practice where pairs of students take it in turns to talk about pictures for one minute each while the rest of the class observes. Their performance can then be discussed.

▶ PART 3

Point out to students how important it is to read the instructions carefully (or listen to them in the exam itself) before they begin. They shouldn't be afraid to discuss how to tackle a particular task, if necessary, since the language used in talking *about* the activity is just as useful to the examiner in assessing candidates as the language used in participating in the activity. Students could usefully practise such expressions as *How shall we start? Are you ready to begin? Shall we make notes? You go first,* etc.

It's also important that students really co-operate to carry out a task. For this reason it would be very useful to revise relevant language for **asking for** and **giving opinions**, and for **agreeing** and **disagreeing** (see Functions Bank pages 105-6).

Practice activities

All the communication activities in this book provide useful practice for this part of the Speaking paper. You can provide extra practice after each activity in this Exam Practice section by asking pairs to team up with another pair to discuss their decisions and reasons.

Near the time of the exam it would be helpful to have a practice session where pairs of students take it in turns to carry out a task while the rest of the class observes, and to have a 'post mortem' afterwards. This will help to get them used to working together under observation and may provide useful reminders to students who speak too much or too little!

▶ PART 4

In this part, the examiner asks more general questions about the topic and encourages a three-way discussion. Again, the language for **giving opinions**, and for **agreeing** and **disagreeing** (see Functions Bank pages 105-6) is important.

Practice activities

Students who have worked through the book should have had plenty of practice in answering questions in this way. For more formal exam practice, arrange students in groups of three; one student with a list of questions acts as the 'examiner' while you monitor the discussions. Afterwards, ask 'examiners' and 'candidates' to report back on the success of the discussions and to mention any problems they experienced. Practise any language areas you feel were weak.

INTERVIEW 1

▶ PART 1

See notes and example questions above.

▶ PART 2

Student 1:
These pictures provide an opportunity to describe the general appearance of the two rooms (one an elegant living room, the other a cluttered but comfortable student's bed-sitting room) and to use vocabulary for furniture and other details.

Discourage students from describing each picture in minute detail. Instead they should move on to mention the main **similarities** (e.g. any furniture they have in common) and **differences**. They must also make it clear which room they prefer and why.

Student 2:
Here there are two kitchens to talk about, one very modern, the other a more traditional farmhouse-style kitchen. There are fewer details to describe and students will need to think about more general points: e.g. Where would you expect to find these kitchens? What kind of people would choose them? What are the advantages and disadvantages of each of them? Again, it is important to explain their personal preference.

▶ PART 3

(See general notes on page 47.) In this task students need to discuss the pros and cons of each activity. Make sure that they have a real discussion and that they ask for and giving opinions. e.g. *Parasailing would be very exciting but it probably wouldn't last very long compared with the other trips. What do you think?* or *I wouldn't choose the glider ride because I'm afraid of flying. How about you?*

Only help students with vocabulary if absolutely necessary since the pictures should give enough information for the task. Ask pairs to report back on their choices and reasons afterwards.

▶ PART 4

See notes on page 47.

INTERVIEW 2

▶ PART 1

See notes and example questions on page 47.

▶ PART 2

Student 1
The two pictures illustrate difference types of game, one a solitary computer game, the other a board game played with friends. Students should **compare** the two types of game (e.g. both provide enjoyment and relaxation but while the computer game is played alone and in silence, the group game is obviously generating a good deal of discussion and humour), and **explain** which of the two would appeal to them most.

Additional points might include: particular games students play and what they enjoy about them; whether it is important to have a winner in a game; games which are educational, etc.

Student 2
Here we see people enjoying two different kinds of entertainment, one an audience watching a film in a cinema (or possible a stage show in a theatre), the other dancers in a discotheque. In Picture 1 there is an opportunity to **describe** the expressions on people's faces (*They look ..., They look as if ..., They seem to be ...,*) and to **speculate** about where they are and what they are watching. In Picture 2, students could talk about the atmosphere and again **speculate** about how it would feel to be there.

Students should mention some **similarities** and **differences**, and **explain** which entertainment they prefer, and why.

▶ PART 3

(See general notes on page 47.) This task will be easier and more realistic if students think of a real teacher to imagine as recipient for the gift. They should think about specific gifts (e.g. what kind of painting? what kind of CDs?) and discuss how appropriate each might be for the purpose and for the teacher in question. They needn't speculate about prices unless they wish to.

Make sure students really ask for and listen to each other's opinions, and that they reach a decision. Be prepared to help with vocabulary if necessary (e.g. *fancy decanter, briefcase*). Afterwards ask pairs to report back on their choices.

▶ PART 4

See notes on page 47.

INTERVIEW 3

▶ PART 1

See notes and example questions on page 47.

▶ PART 2

Student 1
The two pictures show different ways of studying: a child reading a book alone in her room, and students in a school or college library or study room.

Students should **describe** the two scenes, mentioning the girl's expression in Picture 2 and the boy and girl in the foreground in Picture 1. They could also **speculate** about what the girl in Picture 2 is reading and how she feels about it, and what the couple in Picture 1 are doing or saying.

More general points for students to mention might include the advantages and disadvantages of each situation, and how they themselves find they study best (with/without company, with/without music, morning/evening, etc.) and why.

Student 2
The pictures show two different teaching situations. The first shows one-to-one tuition where a student is receiving individual attention from a teacher/tutor. The second shows a teacher working with a small group of pupils in class.

Students should **describe** the two situations and **discuss** the pros and cons of each, drawing on their own experience as far as possible. They could consider the question in relation to different subjects (e.g. mathematics v. a language), and also to different styles of teaching and learning.

▶ PART 3

(See general notes on page 47.) If students reach a decision quickly as to the three most suitable ideas for the magazine, encourage them to discuss these in more detail (e.g. what aspect of culture might be of interest? What kind of competition would be practical?). Make sure there is a balanced discussion and that students reach decisions. Afterwards, ask pairs to report back to the class on their choices of suitable and unsuitable ideas, and their reasons.

▶ PART 4

See notes on page 47.

INTERVIEW 4

▶ PART 1

See notes and example questions on page 47.

▶ PART 2

Student 1

Here students should **describe** in some detail the two contrasting holidays represented by the two pictures. They could focus on various aspects (e.g. food, comfort, cost, convenience, etc.) for **comparison** and they could also consider the kind of people who might find one or other holiday more appealing.

Student 2

The pictures show commuters on a train and a man travelling by car. Students could **describe** the particular scenes briefly but should concentrate on **discussing** the two forms of transport that they represent. Again, they could focus on particular aspects (e.g. cost, convenience, comfort, reliability, pollution, etc.) for **comparison**, and they could perhaps also consider the question in relation to different types of journey (e.g. within a city, in the countryside, long distance).

▶ PART 3

(See general notes on page 47). In this activity students will need to think carefully about each sport in order to assess how suitable it would be for the youth club members to attend. They could consider how popular the sport is, how exciting it is to watch, whether any special knowledge would be needed to undertake it, and so on.

Point out that students must reach agreement on their order of preference. Afterwards, ask pairs to form groups of four in order to compare their results and discuss the reasons for their decisions.

▶ PART 4

See notes on page 47.

INTERVIEW 5

▶ PART 1

See notes and example questions on page 47.

▶ PART 2

Student 1

The pictures represent two approaches to taking exercise. One shows a girl alone in a gym, on an excercise bike; the other shows three friends clearly enjoying their run along the coast. Students should **discuss** the pros and cons of each approach, thinking of cost, convenience, effectiveness, and enjoyment, for example. They could also take into consideration factors like location and weather (running in rainy city streets may not be much fun and may even be dangerous), and also a person's reason for exercising.

Student 2

Here students have to consider two ways of spending a holiday, walking in the open countryside as compared with relaxing on the beach. They can briefly **describe** the scene in the two pictures: in the first, a couple dressed for hiking or trekking (and probably camping) with walking boots and backpacks; in the second someone relaxing with a book in a hammock suspended between two trees. Students should then **discuss** the attractions and drawbacks of each type of holiday, and explain their personal preference.,

▶ PART 3

(See general notes on page 47). Point out to students that in this activity it is the discussion which counts, not guessing the 'right' answer (hair conditioner). They may even think of a more suitable product or service than the original one!

Students are likely to need to use the language of **speculation** (e.g. *It could be advertising makeup./It can't be an advert for jeans.*) and you may consider revising this briefly before they begin the task (See Student's Book p. 188-9).

▶ PART 4

See notes on page 47.

TAPESCRIPTS

UNIT 1 ▶ Taking a break

▶ Focus on listening 1 (p. 12)

A = Travel Agent   B = Client

A Good morning. Can I help you?

B Yes, I wonder if you can give me some information about Crete as a place to go on holiday?

A Of course, what would you like to know?

B Well, I've looked through several brochures and I've picked out four hotels which are about the same price and which sound quite nice. But there's not a lot of information in the brochure and I wondered if you could tell me anything more, because I don't want to end up in a hotel near a discotheque, or where you have to walk five miles to the beach either!

A Right. Well, we have a gazetteer that'll be able to tell us that.

B A what?

A A gazetteer. It's a book which lists all the hotels and describes them, you know. It's supposed to tell the truth. Let me just go and get it!

B Oh, great.

A Now, which hotels were you interested in?

B Let me see, the first one's called the Concord.

A The Concord, right.

B I wondered what sort of building – is it an old style or what?

A Yes, here it is – the Concord. Let's see what it says – a pleasant three-storey building – so it's probably an older type of building, yes. It's about five minutes' walk from the centre of town and a little less from the harbour. Quite a good situation.

B Does it say if it's near the beach?

A Yes. It says it has a terrace at the rear which leads directly on to a beach of sand and rock.

B So I wouldn't have to cross a road to get to the beach?

A No, it leads directly on to the beach, so there's no problem.

B That's fine then. Another one was called the Royal.

A The Royal. Right, yes.

B Yes, that one said that there was a discotheque nearby. I was quite worried about that.

A Right. Let's see what this one says. Yes. It's a three-storey building again, but a modern one. It says it has a curved front. It's also got a good-sized swimming pool and a discotheque situated well away from the bedrooms. So you're not going to be disturbed at night too much.

B Does it say where it is?

A Yes. On a cliff top with steps leading down to a pebble beach. Good bus service to the town centre – so it's obviously a bit out of town.

B Steps down to the beach – well they should keep me fit, I suppose. Fine. Alright. Let's try another one. The Atlantic.

A The Atlantic – strange name for Crete!

B Yes. That one said it was on a main road. That could be noisy, couldn't it?

A Definitely. Right. It's described as a brightly decorated, simple hotel, one of a number recently built alongside the busy main road. There's a picture of it here – look. There are some trees in the front garden which would help to screen it from the road but I'm afraid you're bound to get some traffic noise. It says there's a poor beach opposite but a better one ten minutes' away. So ...

B Well, ten minutes doesn't sound too bad but I don't like the idea of traffic noise. The last one I wanted to ask you about is called the Plaza.

A Right. That's described as a long low building standing high above the main road with an entrance up a steep slope. It's obviously not suitable for elderly or disabled people then. All rooms have balconies and excellent views over the bay. Just a few houses and villas nearby. Hotel transport to the beach.

B That sounds alright. And ... did it say every room had a balcony?

A All rooms have balconies.

B Oh, marvellous! But do you think it would be noisy?

A Well, it says standing high above the main road. So, no I don't think noise would be too much of a problem.

B That's fine then. Now would you be able to give me the price of a flight only?

A Yes, certainly. Let me just get one or two of our flight-only brochures. Right. They have various flights on Fridays and Tuesdays. Now, when do you want to go?

B About the third week in July.

A About the third week. So we're looking at the twenty-first. Tends to be one of the most expensive times to go because that's when the schools break up. Anyway, they go ... they range from £159, all the way up to £191. And that really depends on the flight times.

B OK. And is it advisable to have travel insurance?

A Definitely.

B How much would that cost?

A Roughly ... Well, I can get a leaflet. Hold on. Well, this one ... covers you very very well. It's the most comprehensive policy. And up to two weeks – it's £14.25. This other one we use mainly for students and it doesn't actually cover for cash loss. It's a bit cheaper, though, and that's £10.80.

B Well, thank you very much. That's very helpful. Can I think about it and perhaps call in tomorrow morning?

A Yes. No problem. We're open from 9 till 4 so just pop in any time and we'll see what we can do.

B Right. Thanks very much. Bye.

A OK. Thanks. Bye bye.

▶ Focus on listening 2 (p. 18)

A = Continuity announcer   B = Presenter

A ... And now we come to the programme which gives advice to consumers, *Your Buy*, and here's Mary Simmonds to introduce today's edition.

B Hello, well with the holiday season approaching, we thought it would be a good time to have a look at the subject of suitcases. There are a few people, I know, who use the same old suitcase all their lives. It may be a fine old leather one, covered with labels and stickers from the exotic places they've visited, for example.

Most suitcases, though, don't have quite such a long life and they need to be replaced from time to time. Leather is a bit too expensive to consider these days and it does tend to be rather heavy, too, and for those of us who are looking for something more practical, modern suitcases have a lot of advantages to offer.

In the first place, modern materials like nylon or vinyl can be both extremely tough and yet light enough to carry easily. There are basically two sorts of suitcase – soft ones, made from nylon, vinyl or PVC, and rigid ones, made from materials like ABS or polypropylene.

The second advantage modern suitcases have is that they often offer greater security than the old-fashioned kind. Most have locks or lockable catches of some kind, some have padlocks, and a few even have combination locks to outwit even the most determined thief.

Lastly, most up-to-date suitcases are made with wheels attached so that they can be pulled or pushed instead of carried. Again, there are two main types. Four-wheeled suitcases are designed to be pulled along, parallel to the floor. Suitcases with two wheels are tipped on one end and then either pulled or pushed, using a strap or handle on one side of the case. The four-wheeled sort are more likely to get damaged.

We've chosen four different suitcases to tell you about today. They range in price from the very cheap to the exclusive and expensive!

The first is the Riviera, which is in the middle price bracket. It's 67 cm in length, in smart black PVC with contrasting grey trim. It has four wheels and a towing strap and it was very easy to manoeuvre when we tested it. It's fastened with a medium weight nylon zip, which has a two-year guarantee, and it also has a padlock which gives greater security. It costs £67 and we think it represents good value for money.

The second case, the Windsor, is the cheapest at £32.50 and it's widely available from chain stores all round the country. It's 68 cm long and made of nylon in a choice of three colours and brown trim. There are two wheels and a strap on one side for pushing or pulling it along. It has five separate catches to fasten it and two of these are lockable. All in all it seems good value but the material is not very strong and we thought it might easily get torn.

Our third case is the Tornado and this is made of very tough ABS material in a plain cream colour. It's 75 cm long and has two combination locks, which makes it the most secure of all the cases we tested. If you have a habit of forgetting things like telephone numbers and so on, however, this may not be the case for you! It has two wheels and a metal push-pull handle on the side. The price is £109.50 which may seem high, but you are paying for the added security of that combination lock. Our testers thought it was strong but rather heavy, compared to the first two cases.

The last case we tested is definitely in the luxury price range at £199. It's the Mayfair and is sold only by a few specialist stores, mostly in London. It measures 80 cm and is made of silver-grey aluminium and if you want a case that really stands out from the rest, this is certainly it! It has two locks, though no combination, two wheels and a push-pull handle on the side. We found that it moved very smoothly and easily in our tests and our verdict is that it's both smart and practical but a bit overpriced.

UNIT 2 ▶ Other people's jobs

▶ Focus on listening 1 (p. 23)

Now a look at other courses and career opportunities around this week.

For any unemployed people in the Redfield area, why not try a 'Start' course? They'll be running next week, from the 7th to the 11th of May and are free. The organisers can help out-of-work people get going again by giving advice on retraining, voluntary work and possible jobs.

Hurry, hurry if you want to become Young Engineer of the Year. The closing date for this national competition is the end of May and there's a prize of £1,000 for your school or group if your invention is voted the best in the country.

Well, now to the jobs around this week ... and in Taunton there's a job for a trainee sales person aged between 16 and 18 on business machines. You need a driving licence, either provisional or full – it doesn't matter which – and the pay's £3,000 a year.

In Wells there's a job for two experienced grooms. You'll have to work with four horses in a small showjumping yard. The pay is £40 for a six-day week plus expenses.

At Warmley, there are jobs for twenty shop assistants for a new fruit and vegetable store opening in June. There are five full-time and fifteen part-time vacancies. You've got to be over sixteen and the pay's just over £2 an hour.

And you've got to be an early riser for this next one! It's a trainee baker at Easton. You'll start at six in the morning and they'll pay between £55 and £65 a week.

That's all for this week. The number to ring for any further information is 693217. And happy job hunting!

▶ Focus on listening 2 (p. 35)

A = Interviewer   B = John

A Now, when did you join the Merchant Navy?

B I joined in 1956.

A How old were you then?

B Sixteen.

A Why did you do it?

B I joined because all my family were in the Merchant Navy. My father and all my uncles were merchant seamen, and my brother joined when he was 16, so it was a sort of assumption that I would join the Merchant Navy as well, and it was an idea that I went along with. I never thought of anything else.

A How did it actually start? I mean, where did you ... first join a ship?

B I joined a ship first of all in Tilbury, which is in Essex, after doing six months' training in a ... a training school. And the first ship I joined – in fact, at the last minute they didn't need me. They had enough crew members. And I actually left the ship just before it sailed. Then I was appointed to another ship and ... that time I actually sailed with it.

A And you did a six-month course.

B A six-month course. Yes.

A What sort of things did that cover?

B Very basic things like how to lay a table in a first-class dining room, how to carry cups and saucers and plates when the ship was moving around. But really probably the most important thing and probably one of the reasons they did it was to see whether you were up to being away from home in rather difficult conditions. Because it was a former women's prison that the school was situated in. So it was very spartan with rather ... er ... strict discipline, that sort of thing.

A So what was your title when you first went to sea?

B When I first went to sea, I was a bellboy.

A Would that involve serving as well?

B Well, mainly bellboys used to stand by the bellboard, and then, when one of the bells rang, they went with a silver tray to find out what people wanted.

A How long did you do that for?

B You go up in a series of ranks and the bellboy rating lasts for two years, from the age of 16 to 18.

A And in that first two years did you ever question what you were doing?

B No, never. It never occurred to me. I was too busy enjoying myself, I think.

A Did you ever question your life?

B I only questioned what I was doing when other people questioned me. If somebody said 'You're wasting your time. You could be leading a normal life instead of this sort of gypsy existence of going from place to place all the time.' But it was only for a second because I was earning quite a lot of money and seeing an awful lot of the world.

A How long were you at sea in all?

B I was there till 1962.

A Six years.

B And then I went back to the Merchant Navy for another four years later on.

A Was there ever anything you found really hard to put up with?

B One of the most difficult things was the fact that the living quarters were very poor. And ... em ... the first ship I was on, there were fourteen boys in a cabin, and ... em ... that meant you only had iron bunks and tin drawers that were put underneath the bunks. That was the only furniture in the place, no carpets on the floors, just bare floors. And ... that was a bit grim because, although I must say most of my shipmates were very nice and very good to get on with – if you found somebody that you didn't get on with, it was very difficult because you couldn't get away from them.

A Were you ever in danger – in a dangerous situation?

B Well, it was rather rough on some of those ships. I mean inside the ship if not on the sea! Storms, yes. There was one particular time when the ship ran into a typhoon as we were going into Hong Kong. We weren't allowed into the harbour because it ... em ... the weather was so bad that the ship would've been smashed up against the quay. And I do remember seeing all the heavy anchor chain and such like swept off the front of the ship by a wave, and thinking – well, if you went into the sea in this weather, nothing could save you. We did in fact go in about a day later, into Hong Kong, through into the harbour, and ... em ... I remember there was a ship that had actually been washed up on to the quay. You could actually walk under the bows of the ship!

A Gosh, that must've been quite a storm! What made you decide to leave in the end?

B I left in the end because I'd finally been convinced by people that it was time I did something else. That was really what happened. I mean I would probably have gone on otherwise.

A And did you find another job straight away?

B Well, I went to Australia for six years, I lived there, and then eventually I came back to England and started a completely new career, as you know. But that's another story!

UNIT 3 ▶ Enthusiasms

▶ **Focus on listening 1 (p. 42)**

A = Presenter   B = Liz Jones
C = Bruce McCarthy   D = Barbara Bowen

A Good afternoon. In our programme today, we're going to look at two sports – one well-established, one relatively new. We're also going to hear about those little green birds which most of us have kept as pets at one time or another, but which are a very serious hobby to some people.

Our first report comes from Liz Jones and she's been finding out about the sport of judo.

B Hello. Yes well, I've been visiting a local judo club and I've discovered that judo takes its name from the Chinese term for 'gentle way' though you might not think so when you see the way the club members throw each other about!

Apparently, a Dr Jigoro Kano collected knowledge from the old Japanese samurai jujitsu schools and then founded the first judo school in 1882. The sport has become popular throughout the

world in the last 20 years and there is now an International Judo Federation with its headquarters in Paris. In 1964, judo was first included as an event in the Olympic Games.

The best advice for anyone wanting to take up judo is to contact their nearest large club for information about courses. Membership fees are usually between £16 and £18. You'll need a judo suit and these cost about £15 to buy. You can also hire one from a club for about £5 a month.

A Thank you Liz. And from a sport with an ancient history to one of the world's newest sports – windsurfing. Our reporter is Bruce McCarthy.

C Windsurfing is very simple to describe, but, as I've been discovering, not so easy to do! You first need to learn to balance on a very slim board. Once you've got the hang of that, you have to struggle with a sail that seems to have a mind of its own! Naturally, while you're learning, you fall into the water over and over and over again. And I've got very wet hair to prove it! It's a sport that was invented in 1969 in California (where falling in is a lot more fun, I should think). In 1984 it became an Olympic event and nowadays there are growing numbers of enthusiasts – an estimated 100,000 in Britain, in fact.

If you feel like joining them, you can take a course at a school for between £30 and £40. A beginner's board will cost you around £300 if you decide to buy your own. And, if you really get hooked, a smart racing board will cost at least £1,000.

In Britain the season for windsurfing is from March to September. If you are determined to keep it up during the winter, you'll need a dry suit which you can wear over your ordinary clothes.

A Thanks, Bruce. Now, finally on to that item on a very familiar pet – the budgerigar. Barbara Bowen has been talking to people who keep not one or two but dozens!

D Yes, budgies have come a long way since they were first introduced into this country from Australia around 1840. Nowadays, it's estimated that 1 in 20 households in the UK owns a pet budgerigar, mostly bought from the local pet shop for around £7. Serious budgerigar breeders, on the other hand, will pay £500 for a really successful show bird.

If you're tempted to become a budgerigar breeder, do be warned that although budgies make good tame pets when they're kept singly, they can be quite aggressive when they are mixed together in a group. Most breeders belong to a local society and there's also the Budgerigar Information Bureau which can offer advice on pets and how to breed them. Their telephone number is 01 (if you're outside London) 127 3444. Breeders aim to produce birds of outstanding shape and colour so as to catch the judge's eye at a show. The one bird every breeder would like to be able to produce is a true pink budgerigar but, so far, no one has succeeded!

A Well that's all for today. Hope you can join us next week.

▶ **Focus on listening 2 (p. 51)**

A = Presenter   B = Ned Saunders

A Like a lot of businessmen, Ned Saunders has recently become a lot more concerned about fitness. He started running regularly about two years ago and his current ambition is to run in the next London Marathon.

Ned travels a lot in his work as a Sales Manager and when he attends meetings away from home, he likes to keep up his running while exploring new places at the same time. Last month he was in the city of Bristol for a conference and here he is, describing the route he took on an early morning run.

B I set out to run about five miles on that occasion. It was a typical British summer day – wet and windy! I started from my hotel which was next to the floating harbour and ran up to the statue of Neptune in the City Centre. There I turned sharp left, and keeping the floating harbour on my left, ran past the shops and a boat called the Lochiel which is now a floating restaurant. I then carried on along the north side of the harbour until I was almost opposite the Great Britain, you know – the famous iron ship designed by the engineer Brunel. It's been almost completely restored now and looks magnificent.

At that point, I was forced to turn inland by the road layout. I decided I'd had almost enough of the waterfront anyway, so I headed up Jacob's Wells Road – a gentle climb which forced me to slow down to a jog. The map suggested I needed to go further west so, half way up, I took the first turning on the left – a steep hill as it turned out. Perhaps if I'd realised how steep it was, I'd have found an alternative route! Anyway, by the time I'd struggled to the top I almost stopped off at the nearby Chesterfield Hospital to recover my strength!

The going got easier after that. I carried on past the hospital and took the second turning on the left which led into the heart of pretty Clifton village. From the end of the street, I had a marvellous view of another of Brunel's achievements, the Clifton Suspension Bridge. I fancied going over it and coming back but, as I don't normally carry any money with me when I'm out running, the 2p fee kept me from doing so. Anyway, after I'd stood at the entrance and looked across, I turned round and headed back to town. All downhill and easy going now, I thought.

I passed Clifton Down and ran into Clifton Park. From there I turned right and crossed a busy junction to Richmond Hill. That took me into Queen's Road with all its shops and past the City Museum and Art Gallery. When I reached the University tower, I branched right down Park Street to the City Centre once more.

At the bottom of the hill, it was left past the Hippodrome which had a production of *The Sound of Music*. Then, turning left off the centre, up Colston Street, takes you past the Colston Hall. As Colston Street was taking me uphill again, it seemed as good a time as any to think about turning back. So, it was down Christmas Steps with its little medieval shops and then a dash across the dual carriageway and back via St Stephen's Street to the hotel and a hot bath.

I had been out precisely 43 minutes, including a couple of map reading stops. At a fairly leisurely pace and with a couple of steep hills, about five miles, as I had intended. One of the nicer city runs I've done because there is so much of interest to see in Bristol, even if it is hilly!

UNIT 4 ▶ Lawbreakers

▶ Focus on listening 1 (p. 61)

A = Presenter   B = Detective

A And now we come to the part of our programme where we ask you, the viewer, to help in the fight against crime. Here, to bring us up to date on crime in our area, as usual, is John Haddrell of Wessex CID. Hello John.

B Hello again. Well, first let me thank the viewers for their first class response to our appeal for information last week. You may remember that we told you how thieves had stolen musical instruments belonging to the Barrington Youth Orchestra. Well, I'm glad to say that, thanks to you, those young musicians have got most of their instruments back now.

A Yes, I know you can't tell us too much at the moment, John, but what are the details you can give?

B Well, we managed to locate two flutes, two recorders and a trumpet, following a telephone call from a viewer. Then, a few days later, some more information helped us to trace the rest of the items, with the exception of the drum, which is still missing. Anyway, we're questioning several people at present and we're hopeful of bringing charges quite soon.

A So, on to this week's cases. In the early hours of Monday morning, thieves broke into Bell's toyshop in Regents Road. They took a number of items including a child's bicycle and this doll you can see on your screens now. Is there anything special about it, John?

B Yes, it may look like an ordinary doll but it's actually quite valuable because it's computer-controlled and it's one of only a handful in the country. It's made by an American company and it's got the maker's name 'Computatrix' printed on its back.

A So, if anyone offers you a doll like this at a bargain price, have a look at the back, and if you see that name, get in touch with your local police station. We know the thieves got away in a stolen green van, don't we John? Can you tell us anything about that?

B Well, we still haven't found the green van but we know it was like the one you can see in this picture and the registration was MUG 335J. One other thing, one of the thieves dropped his chequebook and we're hoping that will help us to trace him quite quickly.

A Still on the subject of people who are careless, £5,000 worth of photographic equipment was stolen from Zoom's in the High Street, but look what they left behind!

B Yes, they left the tools they used behind them. You can see some of the items on your screens now. There's a file, a spanner and a rather unusual hammer. Perhaps that'll help to jog someone's memory.

A You're pretty certain that there were three young men involved, aren't you?

B Yes, we've got a pretty good idea that there were three of them, all in their twenties, and we think they were driving a white saloon car of some type but we haven't got any more information on that, I'm afraid.

A Now what about the things they stole?

B Yes, well, they took several cameras, one of which was worth over £1,000. You can see a similar model on your screens now and we're obviously particularly keen to find that. They also got away with quite a lot of professional equipment including tripods, flashguns and telephoto lenses. But the shop also stocks a range of binoculars and telescopes, and the thieves picked one very powerful telescope to add to their haul.

A Well, that's it for this week. If you think you have any information which might help the police to clear up either of the crimes we've told you about, please get in touch with your local police station. Thanks John. See you next week.

▶ Focus on listening 2 (p. 65)

A = Reporter   B = Alan Higgins

A Imagine that you had just got married and then, even before the honeymoon had started, you had your passport, chequebook and all your luggage stolen! What a disaster, you might say. Well, that's exactly what happened to poor Alan and Cheryl Higgins from Southampton. And now they've had to abandon their honeymoon and stay at home in order to sort out all the problems. Earlier today I talked to Alan on the phone and asked him to tell me what happened.

B Well, we were on our way up to the airport to catch a flight to the Canary Islands, where we were going for our honeymoon. And as we had a bit of time in hand, we decided to stop off at Stratford-on-Avon to have a look around. So we parked the car and went for a walk along the river. We can't have been gone for more than 20 minutes, I should say. And when we got back to the car, it had all gone – our two suitcases, and the flight bag which had our airline tickets and passports in it – everything! Oh, and just to make matters worse, the flight bag also had my credit card and our new chequebook in it.

A How did you feel when you saw what had happened?

B I just couldn't believe it. To be honest, I thought it was a joke at first. I thought some of my friends must have followed us up to Stratford and taken the stuff out of the car as a joke. I was expecting someone to jump out from behind a tree, laughing their heads off.

A Where had you left your bags?

B They were all under a blanket. I'd put that over them to hide them. Maybe it just drew the thief's attention to them. But I can't really understand how anybody could do it. I mean, it was obvious that we had just come from a wedding because the car was covered with coloured streamers and someone had written 'Just married' on the back window.

A And when you realised it wasn't a joke, what did you do then? Well, actually, your father's a senior policeman, isn't he, so I suppose you would have known exactly what to do!

B Yes, well we went to the police in Stratford and they were very sympathetic. We gave them all the details but there wasn't much they could do, of course.

A I can see why someone would steal a chequebook but what would they do with your clothes?

B The police said that he'd probably try to sell some of them and then just throw away what he couldn't get any money for.

A Did you have a lot of clothes stolen?

B Yes. All my clothes went. I haven't got anything to wear now except a winter coat. Not much use on a June honeymoon in the Canary Islands!

A What happened then?

B Well, we had to drive back home so as to deal with the insurance and things.

A It can't have been much fun, when you should have been on your honeymoon!

B No, and the trouble is that when something like that happens, you begin to feel afraid even in your own home. But anyway, as Cheryl – my wife – works in a bank, she was able to sort out the problems about the stolen chequebook and the credit cards quite easily. And then we went to the travel agent's, and I must say

they were really marvellous. They managed to fix us up with another holiday in Rhodes in about two weeks' time.

A Oh, so you will be having a honeymoon after all, even if it isn't in the Canary Islands.

B Yes, thanks to them.

A Even so, it must have been an awful experience. How does Cheryl feel about it now?

B Well, she was pretty upset to begin with but now, especially now that the stolen chequebook and credit card have been dealt with, she's a lot happier.

A What a way to start a marriage! After this, are you afraid you're in for a difficult time as a married man?

B Oh no. After all, things can only get better after this! No, it's marvellous to be married.

UNIT 5 ▶ Waste not, want not

▶ Focus on listening 1 (p. 76)

Today we continue our short series about the consumer society with a look at the lifespans of modern products.

Even the best of products wear out in time, of course, but there is a great temptation for manufacturers to design a product so that it wears out quickly even though it could last for years. When our electric light bulb comes to the end of its life after, say, 200 hours, we buy another and the company makes a profit. Bulbs used in factories and industry, however, last much longer and there's no reason why a household bulb shouldn't too.

When things don't wear out fast enough, manufacturers try to persuade customers to buy the latest model by advertising a new style, colour or extra improvements. Of course, real improvements in the design and working of a product are to be welcomed. Very often, however, so called improvements are only minor adjustments or just gimmicks to make you feel that your car or washing machine is out of date. The fashion and car industries have been most successful at this game of introducing new models on a regular basis. But manufacturers of household goods and furniture have been trying to cash in too. If manufacturers have their way the kitchen of tomorrow will be bought as a single unit. There will be yearly model changes and a range of colour schemes so that your kitchen matches the disposable chairs, plates and cutlery you'll be using in it!

In the developing world, the story is rather different. Products which we take for granted are scarce and they have to last much longer. If they break or break down, they are patched or repaired to keep them going for as long as possible.

Washing machines and irons, for example, are designed by their makers to have a useful life of 5 years and that is the length of time that they are normally used for in the USA. In underdeveloped countries, however, they go on being used for 5 times as long – for 25 years, in fact.

Another example is that of cars. They are designed to last 11 years but in America they are replaced with a newer model after an average of only 2.2 years. In the third world they are often kept going for 40 years or more.

The figures for bicycles are even more astonishing. Bicycles, like cars, are only used for about 2 years even though they are designed by their makers to have a useful life of 25 years. In developing countries bicycles are so valuable that they go on being used for up to 75 years!

In the case of another vital product, construction equipment, the makers estimate that this will have an average useful life of 14 years. In the USA it is usually replaced after only 8 years but in the third world, construction equipment is still in use in many places after 100 years or more.

Ships are kept in use for almost as long – 80 years in fact, in the third world, compared with America where they have a working life of only 15 years – just half the time they are designed to last by their manufacturers.

A final example is that of photographic equipment which is designed to last for 35 years and continues to be used for 50 in underdeveloped countries. The shocking fact is that Americans replace their cameras and other equipment after an average of just over one year, or 1.1 years, to be exact!

I think these figures speak for themselves. The fact is that a small proportion of the total population is using too many of the world's resources and using them terribly wastefully. The situation can't continue for ever because the world's resources are shrinking fast.

▶ Focus on listening 2 (p. 84)

    A = American tourist   B = Tourist information officer

Part one

A I'm a visitor to Britain and I'm very interested in your national parks. I'd like to ask you a few questions about them if I may.

B Well, I'll do my best to answer them.

A How many are there altogether?

B Ten.

A And how were they originally set up?

B Well, during the Second World War people were getting more and more interested in the idea of national parks. The first national parks had been created in the United States back in the 19th century, as you probably know ...

A Yeah, I'm from California myself.

B And that had created worldwide interest. So after the war the government finally acted and a law was passed in 1949 to create a new body called the National Parks Commission.

A And were all the ten parks created at that time too?

B No. The first four were set up two years later in 1951. Then more were added up until 1957, when the last national park was created.

A And what kind of places are they, these national parks? I mean, in the States they're pretty wild, but I guess you don't have any real wildernesses in Britain.

B No, very few. But they are all very different. To give you some idea, perhaps I'd better describe one or two.

A I'd appreciate that. I'm hoping to get to see some during my visit.

B Well, let's take the Lake District which is the best known ...

A Sure, I've heard of that.

B It's the largest of the national parks and it's got some marvellous lake and mountain scenery – including Scafell Pike which is the highest mountain in England. It's very popular with visitors especially as some of the lakes can be used for sailing, canoeing and swimming, and the mountains are ideal for rock climbing.

A What about the Peak District? It's shown right in the middle of the map I have here. It sounds like there are mountains there too.

B Well, no – despite the name, there aren't many peaks there in fact. There are really two Peak Districts – the White Peak and the ...

A Why's it called that?

B Oh, it's called the White Peak because of the white-coloured limestone. And then there's also the Dark Peak which is more dramatic but still beautiful. The Peak District gets about 2 million visitors a year, you know, which makes it the most heavily-used of all the national parks.

A Is there a special reason for its being so popular?

B Well, as I said, it is very beautiful, but I think it's also because just about half the population of England lives within a day trip of the Peak District, so it's quite easy to get to.

A I see. Which is the smallest of the parks?

B The Pembrokeshire Coast is. It's in the south-west of Wales – can you see it on the map? It's also the most densely populated of the parks. It's a really beautiful coast – I'd recommend you to go there. It's got a mild climate and there are lovely walks along the cliff tops.

A OK – you've persuaded me! And if I decide to head for Wales, I guess I could also go to the Snowdonia National Park. What is there to see there?

B Well, Snowdon of course! That's the highest mountain in England and Wales, and well worth a visit. But there's lots more. It's got beaches, too, as you can see from the map, and forests, lakes and waterfalls. There are quite a number of historic houses and castles ...

A Castles?!

B Oh yes, and old mines too if you're interested in industrial archaeology.

A Great! I have to go there. Now tell me about Northumberland. That's on the border with Scotland, isn't it?

B Yes, and it's in one of the most remote areas of the country. You can wander for miles and hardly ever see another person.

A But isn't Hadrian's Wall in Northumberland? I've heard that's quite something.

B Yes, that's in the south of the park and that's where most of the visitors go. It was a wall built by the Romans to keep the Scots out and it's a very important and impressive site.

Part two

A Well, thank you for all that information. One last question: can you explain those signs on the wall to me? There are ten of them so I guess they must represent the ten national parks.

B That's right. Most of them are designed to show some special feature of the park. For example, the one with the pony on it ...

A Pony? Which is that? My eyes aren't too good.

B Can you see? – the one shaped like a diamond – with a black pony, a small horse, on it.

A Oh yes – now which park is that for?

B That's the sign for Dartmoor because of the famous Dartmoor ponies which wander over Dartmoor. Exmoor, on the other hand, has a lot of wild deer and the sign for Exmoor shows a stag's head. It's that triangular one over there. Can you see it?

A The triangular one, you say? Right! I've got it.

B Yes, and you can see the stag's head with its wide antlers branching out on top. Now can you see the white bird on a black background?

A Yeah, I can see a bird – with long wings – flying. What is it? An eagle?

B I'm not sure, to tell you the truth. Anyway it's the sign for Northumberland National Park.

A Northumberland? That's one I'm planning to go to. Tell me, is that some kind of sheep – there in the square sign?

B Yes it is. Well, it's meant to be a ram's head actually! It's the sign for the Yorkshire Dales, because Yorkshire is great sheep-rearing country. Can you see the ram's fine curling horns?

A Sure. Now, that one with a mountain – is that the sign for the, er, Lake District?

B Which one with a mountain? There are two ...

A The circular one – there's a mountain in the distance and, I guess it's a lake, in front.

B Correct! It's the Lake District. But can you guess what the one with the fire is?

A Let me see ... fire ... no, wait a minute. It's not the Brecon Beacons, is it?

B   You're absolutely right. Well done! As you know, beacons were fires lit at the top of hills as a kind of signal, and hills where that happened are sometimes called 'beacons' too.

A   OK. That makes sense. But the one that really foxes me is that thing like modern art. The one with the circle on the rectangle. What on earth is that supposed to represent?

B   I'm afraid I'm as baffled as you are. I can tell you it's the sign for the Peak District.

A   Well, thanks again. I won't take any more of your time but I've learned a lot today, and I'm looking forward to seeing a couple of national parks for myself! By the way, if you're ever in California, I can recommend the Yosemite National Park!

UNIT 6 ▶ The shape of things to come

▶ Focus on listening 1 (p. 93)

C = Reporter   A = Anne Evans
B = Nigel Floyd   D = Jack Daniels   E = Mary Silver

A   As far as I'm concerned, it's about the third worst thing that's happened in my life. I can't – I honestly can't imagine anything worse, except illness or death!

B   I've never lived through a more terrible moment in my life. It was then about midnight and I was alone in the house. I simply sat in the chair and covered my head with a cushion and wished I were a long way away where no one could find me.

C   What on earth was the tragic disaster in these people's lives? The end of their marriage? The loss of their job? Had the dog run away? Actually, they're all writers and they'd lost extremely important work in their word processors. And, as Nigel Floyd, the cookery writer explains, when your computer lets you down, it can be just as bad as a broken love affair!

B   I'd finally got round to investing in a word processor and it had taken me quite a bit of time to get used to it. But it was proving really useful and I began to think of it as an old friend! I was about half way through the book when I decided to change one of the recipes, so I put in the disk and found the place. Then, without thinking, I pressed the key but it must have been the wrong one because, instead of just deleting part of the recipe, the whole disk was wiped clean and I had lost 50 recipes, about five days' work. I couldn't believe it. And after that, I'm afraid I went back to my old typewriter – much more reliable!

C   And as journalist Anne Evans explains, pressing the wrong key is not the only thing that can destroy your work ...

A   I'd just got back from New York and I was writing an article which was going to be a main feature in the newspaper I work for, a world exclusive in fact. I only had the night to write it – the deadline was in the morning. I worked all night in my office on an Astra computer. And I got the article finished! Then, at 7 o'clock in the morning, in comes the cleaning lady, takes out the plug and puts in her vacuum cleaner! This cut off all the electricity and all my work had gone! The whole article! I had two hours before the deadline ...

C   Just switch off the electricity or press the wrong button and your trusted work mate can change into a technological monster! Here, with another horror story, is novelist, Jack Daniels.

D   I was working on a novel which was giving me quite a lot of trouble. I'd been correcting and rewriting the first two chapters for nearly a month, using my old Rocket 22. Anyway, finally I finished the first two chapters – very late. Then I decided to copy what I'd written on one disk on to another, for safe keeping. I pressed the right key – no question about that – and then I thought I'd just check to make sure the machine had copied what I wanted it to copy. And, to my horror, I found that it had stored only some of my very early notes, and the rest of my work – two whole chapters – had been completely lost. It was the absolute end!

C   But even without errors and malfunctions, your life's work is still not entirely safe stored in a computer. As Mary Silver, the television reporter, tells us.

E   I'd been doing research for a very long and very important television documentary on the American elections. I'd spent several weeks travelling in the States, interviewing people, and I had an enormous amount of material. I'd completed three days' very intensive work of putting together historical details and facts and statistics, and it was nearly finished. Anyway, I was working late one night and I felt I just couldn't do any more, so I decided to give myself four hours' sleep, so I went to bed. Everybody was in – my husband, the three children. And, er, I came down at about seven in the morning to find broken glass everywhere. It was obvious what had happened. And my word processor had disappeared. And with it had disappeared my entire script for the documentary.

C   And what was your reaction?

E   Well, absolute horror! I couldn't understand why they'd stolen the word processor because the only other thing they'd taken was a frozen chicken from the freezer, and I couldn't see the connection between the frozen chicken and the American elections!

▶ Focus on listening 2 (p. 96)

A = Presenter   B = Child 1   C = Child 2
D = Child 3   E = Child 4   F = Child 5   G = Child 6

A   Twenty years ago we asked a group of thirteen-year-olds what they thought life would be like in the year 2000. And this is what they said ...

B   In the year 2000, I think I'll probably be in a spaceship on my way to the planet Mars. Or else I may be in charge of a robot court, judging some robots. Or I may be at the funeral of a computer. Or, if something's gone wrong with someone's nuclear bombs, I may be coming back to my cave from a hunting trip!

C   I think the population will have gone up so much that either everyone will be living in big plastic domes in the Sahara desert or else they'll be living under the sea.

D   Computers are taking over now. Computers and automation. And in the year 2000 there just won't be enough jobs to go around.

A   Well that was before the manned moon landing, the microprocessor and test-tube babies. So, have the hopes and fears of today's thirteen-year-olds changed as they look forward to the year 2020? We asked a second group of children and here are some of their answers.

E   Obviously nuclear war worries me, but I don't think that'll happen. Unless they've got computers that press the button for them. Because I don't think that any human being can – is capable of actually pressing some button that releases all the nuclear arms. 'Cos it would just mean the destruction of the world.

F   Perhaps we'll be able to convert brain waves into radio waves and then change them back to brain waves, so you could actually have a conversation with someone without talking. But you'd have to be able to stop them understanding some of your thoughts I suppose in case they got upset! And there'll be so many people – I think there may – unless they have another planet to go to – there'll be loads and loads of tower blocks for people to live in, or people will be restricted to a certain number of kids.

G   It'll probably be computers that are running the country by then. I mean they're beginning to now and that can be a good thing. But when it comes to war and things like that – nuclear bombs, and they're designing gases that can kill people within seconds. I think that aspect of technology should be wiped out completely.

A   Amazing, isn't it? Twenty years later and yet the issues remain the same.

UNIT 7 ▶ Going the hard way

▶ Focus on listening 1 (p. 132)

A = Interviewer   B = Prospective traveller

A   Just tell me what happens, then. You set off, on Thursday, in a coach, a car ...?

B   Well, you go by coach to Dover and then on the other side, they've got a, the company has specially converted double-decker buses.

A   Oh really?

B   So the bus picks you up, at Calais I think it is, and then you go on the bus all the way to Kathmandu. So it takes about ten weeks.

A   And what's the route actually?

B   Um – you go down through Europe to ... well, you go through Venice and then down through Greece and Turkey, um, and then from Turkey you go down through Syria and Jordan. Then you go back up through Syria and Jordan again and back into Turkey. And from Turkey you go to Iran and then you go across Iran and, um, into Pakistan. And up through northern India and finally into Nepal. You go to Kathmandu and stay there for about a week or ten days.

A   U – hum. And did you have to get all the visas for the various places?

B   Well, I had to get three. I had to get an Australian visa, an Indian visa and an Iranian visa.

A   Do you have to have supplies of money for each place? – I mean local currency?

B   Well no. What I've done is just to get a lot of traveller's cheques – plus they advise you to take some dollars in cash because, well, that's acceptable currency in a lot of places. So it's just a case of changing the money as you get into a new country.

A   And do you sleep on the bus?

B   Yeah. They've converted the top deck so you sleep there. And downstairs there's seating and, um, a sort of kitchen.

A   And how rough is it?

B   I don't think it's too bad. They've got bunk beds with mattresses and you take a sleeping bag. And I think the hotels they provide are quite adequate. There are quite a few overland companies and with a lot you have to camp every night. Well, I mean camping's fine for a couple of weeks, but four months! And having to travel all day and then stop and pitch tent! At least this way, if you get tired during the day, you can just go upstairs and have a lie down.

A   Do you know anyone who's going?

B   No.

A   Is there an age limit?

B   Yes, 35. It's 18 to 35.

A   Do you get a lot of information before you go?

B   Oh, yes. They send you a list of things you should do, about how to get the visas and about your injections because you have to have lots of vaccinations, and what clothes to wear ...

A   Well, you can't take much luggage, can you?

B   No, well I've just got a fairly small travel bag and I'll take a rucksack as well, so that, um, I can pack everything in and I've also got some space for souvenirs and things.

A   So you sleep on the bus all the way to Kathmandu, and then you stay in a ...

B   Hotel. Yes. After Kathmandu, it's a mixture of buses and planes and trains. It's all local transport and you stay in hotels.

A   I see.

B   You actually fly from Kathmandu to Burma.

A   Well, how much does it all cost?

B   Well – the actual trip from London to Australia costs just over £2,000. It seems a lot but it's for four months' travel and that includes your hotel accommodation. Well, all your accommodation. And transport, and food. So really all you've got to take is your spending money.

A   What made you want to do it?

B   Well, I've always wanted to go round the world and before now I've never really had the money. I've been working for the last few years so I've managed to save up the money and I thought it's a good time to do it. I'm not too young and I'm not too old and ...

A   How old are you?

B   I'm twenty-four. I don't own a house or anything like that, that it might be difficult to leave behind. And I just thought I might as well do it now while I've got the chance.

A   It's very brave! And what will you do in Australia?

B   I don't know but I've got some friends in Brisbane I'm going to stay with and I've got a work permit for six months so I might be able to pick up some work. Um. So I really just want to have a look around. I'd like to go to New Zealand as well.

A   Well it all sounds fantastic! I'm quite envious actually – anyway, best of luck and don't forget to send me a postcard.

B   I won't.

▶ Focus on listening 2 (p. 141)

A = Interviewer   B = David Hempleman-Adams

A   Well, I've been looking forward to meeting you and I'm longing to ask you about your walk to the North Pole. It was, well tell me, was it three years ago that you went?

B   The first expedition was to the geographical North Pole and that was 1982 and that was a couple of years' planning, so the initiation of that first expedition was probably 1980 and then it took a long time to plan it, and then we finally left England in 1982 and got up into the north of Canada in February.

A   Sorry, was that the first trip or the second?

B   The first trip.

A   The first trip, yes. Did that ... was that successful?

B   No. We ... at the time, I got to 87°11` and I cracked three ribs and I gave up after ... um ... a bit of soul searching. And it was a bit disappointing in some respects because there'd been a lot of planning and although we failed ... it was good in the sense that we did so well because everyone said we'd be ... or I would be dead in six days because of the cold, and so it was interesting that I actually succeeded in living in those conditions for 42 days and actually achieved about three quarters of the distance. And at that time it was the furthest anyone had attained, getting to the North Pole without dogs or snowmobiles.

A   Yes. After that first one, didn't it put you off starting again to do a second visit?

B   Yes, um ... At the time ... it's like anything that ... which, when you're in conditions where you're extremely frightened and it's dangerous, you feel what on earth are you doing here, I mean, it's crazy and every minute I hated it but when I was home, I missed it completely – so it was something that I had to get back to, and as the months passed, I – I wanted to get back ... and try it again. At that stage I was trying to emulate what had happened in the Himalayas, and that was small alpine expeditions, they're becoming smaller and smaller on big mountains. And that culminated in Ronald Messner climbing Everest solo without oxygen and that to me was the purest form of ...

A So that's what attracts you really, is the refining it to its simplest form?

B Yes, well, in this day and age, I mean, I've been born in the twentieth century and unfortunately everything's been explored ... um ... so really the only thing that's left to myself and other explorers ... is to try and do it better or faster or on less money, or more refined, as you say. There'd always been these massive dog teams – twenty or thirty dog teams ... and airplane support which used to cost millions of pounds, in fact, and to me there was no correlation between the amount of money that you paid into an expedition and the success of it. So I thought, well, what's the point of spending millions and not succeeding, if you could do it in a lightweight fashion – just go with a sledge, without dogs or air support – it would be cheaper and if you failed then you could have another go.

A Yes.

B So I failed the first time and that was with air support ... I was having a drop every twelve or sixteen days. The second expedition, I wanted to go back and try and push it a stage further and try and be the first person to reach the North Magnetic Pole but that would be in, again, the purest form of travel, without the use of dogs or snowmobiles, but in addition without any air support whatsoever. So everything that I took ... that was, um, completely a survival kit for myself. And the second expedition, I was very fortunate, um ... and I ... with the experience of the first expedition, I achieved that trip.

A And ... did you have any really frightening moments during this trip?

B I think every day was frightening because at the end of the day, you didn't know if you were ever going to get home ...

A Um ... no, what about polar bears?

B Well, ... the first trip I saw one but I didn't actually have any problems. But I had this theory that on my second trip, because I was coming down – it was a bit further south – and I was going through migration routes for polar bears ... and we knew polar bears liked Mars bars, so what I did, I used to put a sledge about 20 feet away from the tent in line with the tent flap, and put Mars bars on top of the sledge. And one night, I was asleep and I heard this rustling and this polar bear was after the Mars bars and ... the next thing I know, it was rolling me out of the tent, and ...

A Sorry, why did you put the Mars bars out?

B Well, I knew that if it went for the Mars bars first that would give you a couple of seconds to wake up and try to get your gun because, I mean, two or three seconds was crucial. And so this thing came straight for the tent while I was trying to get out of it, and ... I shot a ... there's a theory that polar bears are more scared of noise rather than shooting ... so I shot a round through the floor just to scare it, and it did scare it about twenty feet, and then I gave it another two warning shots, and then it just started to charge, and so I had to try and stop it.

A Really?

B I was really upset by it all, and ... um ... seeing this thing coming towards me really unnerved me. And so I got, we got the plane

in and sent it back to Resolute and we gave it to the community. They're not endangered at all and they're not protected at all up there. Resolute has a quota of polar bears a year they can kill and so it just came off that quota.

A Which upset you? Was it, um, the narrow escape from death or was it shooting the animal?

B Shooting the animal.

A Was it?

B Because I felt it was fair game that he could come after me because I was in his environment and I felt that I was going home after the expedition. But that was his environment and I felt that it was unfair for me to ... although it's the survival of the fittest, I thought it was a shame because they're beautiful animals and I think that if anyone should appreciate that environment, it's probably polar bears more than, more than me.

UNIT 8 ► Family life

► Focus on listening 1 (p. 153)

A = Adult   B = Child 1   C = Child 2   D = Child 3

A Right, we'll start with you then. Can you tell ... can you tell us how old you are?

B Nine.

A Nine. And have you got brothers and sisters?

B Yeh.

A How many?

B Two brothers.

A Two brothers. Are they older than you?

B No, younger.

A What about pocket money? Do you get some pocket money?

B Um, sometimes. We get about ... off my nan I get about ... five pounds thirty.

A Five pounds thirty! What, every week?

B No. Three pounds fifty, I mean.

A What, every week?

B Well, most of the time, I don't get it very often, though.

A Um. What do you do with it when you do get it? What do you spend it on?

B I spend it on things like ... well, sweets and that.

A Is that why one of your teeth has gone, there? Is it?

B Yeh, it's come out.

A And you don't get pocket money from your mummy for helping in the house?

B No, usually my mum gives me about 5p for doing the washing up and laying the table and that.

A And how often do you do that?

B Nearly every day.

A Nearly every day. Who does it when you don't do it, then?

B My ma has to do it, because I'm at school most of the time.

A Ah, do you have to give her 5p then, when she does it?

B No.

A No! Oh. How much pocket money do you think you'd like to have?

B About ... ten pounds.

A Right. Now, you've got ten pounds a week. What would you spend it on?

B Um ...

A Not more sweets?

B Um ... toys.

A And what about when you're naughty? What does mummy do when you're naughty?

B Oh ... ooh ... she just sends us up to bed, sometimes.

A Sometimes. And what does she do other times?
B She gives us a smack.
A Oh, does it hurt?
B Mmm.
A So you're not naughty very much?
B No. Try not to be.
A Um?
B Try not to be.
A Try not to be. No. What time do you go to bed usually?
B About half past nine.
A Every night?
B Well, on a ... well, on a Friday and Saturday I go to bed at about eleven o'clock, when my ma goes to bed.
A Oh. Do you watch a lot of television?
B Um ... most of the time, yeh.

A Now, how old are you?
C Seven.
A Seven. Have you got brothers and sisters?
C Yes.
A How many?
C Two.
A What, brothers or sisters?
C One girl and one boy.
A And are they smaller or bigger than you?
C Bigger.
A Oh. And what about your pocket money? How much pocket money do you have?
C Fifty pence.
A Fifty pence. And who gives you that?
C My mum.
A And what do you do with it then?
C Put it in my money box, or spend it on something when I, um, want some sweets or something.
A And would you like to have more pocket money?
C Umm. Ten pound.
A You'd like ten pounds. You're going to have to tell me what you'd spend your ten pounds on.
C I'd like to buy loads and loads of soft toys.
A Would you? And put them all in your bedroom?
C Yeh. I love soft toys.
A Fill your bed up so you can't get in any more? Um. Thought so. What time do you go to bed?
C About eight o'clock or nine o'clock.
A Is it later at the weekends?
C Umm. Yes. Ten o'clock at the weekends.
A Ten o'clock at the weekends.
C Umm. Or nine o'clock.
A And what do you do when you stay up so late? Do you watch television?
C Sometimes. Sometimes I'm still out playing.
A And what about when you're naughty? What happens then?
C I get sent up in my bedroom.
A And who does that most? Mummy or daddy?
C Dad.
A Does he? Oh. And do you have to help in the house?
C Umm. A lot.
A What do you have to do?
C Washing up, dusting, wiping up, putting away, um ... and loads more things.
A What happens if you drop mummy's best plates?
C I get sent to bed.
A And what about when you grow up and get married? Do you want to have children?
C Yeh.

A How many would you like to have?
C Six.
A Six! Gosh, you'd need a big house. Why six?
C Oh, don't know.
A Have you found a boyfriend who wants six as well?
C No.

A Right. Can we start by asking you how old you are?
D Eight.
A Eight. And do you live at home with mummy and daddy and brothers and sisters?
D Yes.
A How many brothers and sisters?
D Um, I haven't got any brothers and sisters but I live at home.
A Just you on your own with your mum and dad?
D Yeh, but mum's having a baby in two weeks' time.
A Oooh. Are you excited about that?
D Yes.
A And what about pocket money? Do you get pocket money from your parents?
D Yes.
A How much do you get?
D Um, sometimes I get two pounds, but mostly I get one pound, from all the family.
A And what do you do with it? What do you spend it on?
D Um, toys.
A What sort of toys?
D Um, Care Bears.
A Care Bears? And what do you do with all these Care Bears?
D Um, put them in my bedroom, cuddle them at night.
A All night?
D Yes.
A Umm. And do you think you get enough pocket money?
D Yeh, 'cause my mum said if I had too much I wouldn't know what to buy with it and I agree with her.
A Oh. And do you have to help in the house to get your pocket money, or ...?
D No.
A But do you help in the house?
D Sometimes.
A What do you do then?
D Um, lay the table, bring the knives and forks, make some drink ...
A And what happens when you're naughty?
D Oh, I get smacked.
A By whom?
D My dad, usually.
A Does it hurt?
D No.
A That's a waste of time then.
D When he's really angry he does.
A I see. So you've got to make him really angry. And what about going to bed? What time do you go to bed?
D Um, my latest is eleven o'clock and my earliest is eight o'clock.
A And what do you do until you go to bed?
D Um, watch the telly and read books.
A And what do you do when you stay up till eleven o'clock?
D Um, it's usually to watch films.
A And if it's eight o'clock and there's a nice film on, do you stay up to watch it?
D No, I usually watch EastEnders, when it's on.
A And then go to bed?
D Yes.
A Good. And what about when you grow up and get married? Do you want to have children?

D Yes.
A How many would you like to have?
D Two.

▶ Focus on listening 2 (p. 159)

H = Helen   G = Gay

H It's Gay, isn't it?
G Yes. Hallo.
H It's Helen. Do you remember me?
G Yes, yes. Haven't seen you for ages.
H God, it must be years! How are you?
G I'm fine. How are you? You look well.
H Well, I've just been on holiday. What are you doing these days?
G Well, I'm doing some part-time teaching.
H And how's Dick?
G Oh, we're not together any more. He left about three years ago, I'm afraid.
H Oh my God, that must be difficult for you.
G Well, it is sometimes – it's not too bad.
H Have you got any children?
G Yes, I've got a daughter, 13. Gosh! I haven't seen you for a long time! – a daughter, Lily, who's 13, and a 5-year-old boy.
H My God! How do you cope? Have you people around who help you?
G Well, I'm very lucky. I've got a very supportive group of women friends and we share the child care. I mean it's difficult sometimes – when you go out, you've got to pay for going out and pay for a baby-sitter, that sort of thing.
H But what about clothes and shoes? That must be terrible.
G Well, my mother-in-law's very good. She buys the children shoes. And I don't mind wearing jumble sale clothes and cheap clothes.
H I bet she doesn't buy you clothes! Do you find then that you find it difficult to meet people yourself?
G No, I'm very lucky round here. It's very friendly, and just working part-time is very helpful.
H Where do your family live? Do they live here too?
G Well, no. I've got three brothers – they're all in London. And my father who's 82 is down in Hampshire.
H So you've got to look after him as well?
G Well, I've got to go down about every four weekends or so to see if he's OK. But luckily he's in quite good health. Cheerful. And the kids love going down there.
H How on earth do you manage to make ends meet?
G Well, I get some help. I don't think it's enough really. I think, on the whole, fathers get off rather lightly.
H Because he had quite a good job, didn't he?
G Oh yes, he's a dentist. It's difficult really. If I ask him for more money, it makes things difficult, so I prefer, on the whole, to keep a good relationship with him for the children. They go and spend a night with him once a week, but I don't really think that's doing enough. You know, I have to do all the disciplining and going to parents' evenings and ...
H He buys them ice cream.
G That's right. And he buys them nice expensive presents. So, it's a bit uneven I think.
H So – what kind of teaching are you doing?
G Well, I haven't actually been doing any teaching for six months. I've been doing a wonderful course. It's a wood-machining course.
H A what?
G A wood-machining course. It's been really good fun.
H Whatever's that?

G Well, it's partly funded by central European funds. And it's for women only. And it's been six months and I hope I'm going to set up doing jobs as a wood worker. I've already been asked to make a wardrobe and a plate rack and ...
H What a wonderful idea!
G shelves, and I think it'll be much better than teaching. I really enjoy doing it. It's practical. And the course is so good. You get ...
H Did you have to pay for it?
G No, it was free. And what's even better, there's child care provision built into it. So it means that I can actually, it means that Lily can collect Finn after school on the three days that I've been doing it. And there's money to pay her a reasonable allowance.
H So they pay childcare for you to have a baby-sitter or a child-minder, and you gave it to her instead. That's a good way of keeping the money in the family!
G Well, yes – it means she helps and she doesn't resent helping. Yes, it's been very good.
H I suppose she's quite independent.
G She is. I think on the whole both my children are very independent. I think maybe that's one of the positive aspects of single parenting. I notice that they're very outgoing and they're very easy, they make friends very easily with adults and with other children.
H I suppose they're used to having different child-minders and going to nursery school from when they were quite young?
G Yes, they've never been at all clinging. They've been quite happy to go off and go with other people. They're very independent, both of them.
H Well, that's one good thing that's come out of it then.
G Yes it is.

UNIT 9 ▶ Looking after yourself

▶ Focus on listening 1 (p. 166)

A = Presenter   B = Expert

A We all know the old saying 'An apple a day keeps the doctor away'. I suppose there's absolutely no truth in that?
B Well, actually I wouldn't say there's no truth in it. It's like a lot of so-called old wives' tales and advice our grandmothers used to give us – we used to laugh but medical discoveries can prove them right after all. Anyway, apples are certainly a good source of fibre, and fibre, as we now know, is an important element in our daily diet. Apart from that, apples contain Vitamin C which helps build up resistance to disease. So there are some good reasons for eating apples regularly, but I wouldn't like to promise that they'll protect you from all ailments so the saying is a bit of an exaggeration. In any case, there's a great deal more Vitamin C in oranges.
A Right, well what about the advice to always sleep with an open window? I had an uncle who believed it firmly and who stuck to the rule right through the depths of winter!
B Well, I'm afraid that is a myth, and a dangerous one at that. Old people are much more likely to catch infections in extreme cold and that's true of babies too. Cold air can irritate a cough and make life much more uncomfortable for people who suffer from bronchitis. Personally, I wouldn't recommend anyone to leave the window open in cold weather – after all, if you're worried about the bedroom getting stuffy, you can always leave the door open to let the air circulate.

A   Yes, well that's good advice. Another thing you often hear is that if you get wet through, you're more likely to catch a cold. I must say I've always believed that.

B   Yes, a lot of people do, but actually there's no evidence whatsoever to prove it. There have been experiments both in Britain and America and the results were the same in both countries. Volunteers stayed in damp clothes for some time but they developed no more colds afterwards than their fellow volunteers who had stayed dry. There was also the case of a man in Norway who fell into a freezing river during the spring thaw. He'd spent the winter completely alone – he was a trapper I think. Anyway, he didn't catch a cold as a result, even though he'd had to spend hours in his wet clothes. Then, a few weeks later, he was back in contact with other human beings and he quickly caught a streaming cold!

A   Well that's quite surprising, I must say. Another myth bites the dust! Now, what about the saying 'Feed a cold and starve a fever'? I've always found that seems to work.

B   Of course it does! People often have quite hearty appetites right through a cold, but when you've got a high temperature you don't feel much like eating. So it's obvious really. On the other hand, if you've got a high 'flu temperature, you need to drink plenty of liquid to replace the fluid you lose through sweating.

A   And the last piece of old wives' wisdom I wanted to ask you about is that carrots help you to see in the dark. I seem to remember that someone once died from drinking too much carrot juice, didn't they?

B   Yes, that's right but it was a man who drank enormous quantities – more than any normal person would dream of consuming. In fact carrots are a very good source of carotene, and that's a substance which is converted in the body to Vitamin A. Vitamin A is vital because it enables the eye to adapt so that you can see in twilight and darkness. Night blindness is a common symptom of Vitamin A deficiency. There are other good sources of Vitamin A apart from carrots, though – green beans for example, milk, butter, and also fish oils.

▶ Focus on listening 2 (p. 173)

Well, if everyone's here, perhaps I'd better make a start. The course you're taking is ... a ... a basic first aid course. We meet once a week on a Tuesday afternoon and the whole course is 20 hours. At the end, you'll take an exam and, if you're successful, you'll get an official certificate to prove that you're a qualified first aider.

As you might expect, there will be a fair amount of practical work during the course because first aid is a subject where a little practical experience is worth a lot of theory! Some of you may be a bit worried about whether you'll be able to put bandages on correctly as you've seen in a first aid handbook. Well, let me reassure you. You can be quite a competent first aider even if you're not very good at putting on bandages. On the other hand, you ... you can be ... er ... a better first aider, shall we say, a more effective first aider, if you're prepared to do the necessary overtime. In other words, to do some extra practice at home following the demonstrations you see during the course.

Now, the first thing you have to remember about first aid, above all else, is this: the need for first aid comes when you least expect it! There are times when extremely fast action can save a life. Now, I'll give you one example of that kind of situation.

I was in a restaurant, having a meal. A gentleman was over there, having a meal. We were taking no notice of each other. Quite suddenly, while I was in the middle of my meal, there was a noise from his table. And I looked over – he'd brought his hands down heavily on the table and he was obviously in some kind of difficulty. I watched him for a moment and he was now leaning forward over the table as if he was in pain. So I got up from my seat and walked

across – ten metres, five metres, something like that – to him and noticed, as I got to him, that a section of his false teeth, his denture, was lying at the side of the plate, on the table cloth. And I looked at him and he was now purple, purple! He couldn't breathe. There was something in his throat and it was totally blocking his airway.

By this time, a waiter had come in and said, 'What's the matter?' and I said, 'I want to get this man lying across his chair so that he's facing the floor.' So, with the waiter's help, I got him lying over the chair. And I shouted to the waiter, 'Call an ambulance! Now.' Because sometimes people get terrified in this kind of situation. They've got to be pushed to know what to do. So he followed my command to go and call an ambulance.

Now, with this man, his airway had to be cleared of the obstruction. I had to get that piece of denture out. Otherwise he was going to die. Now I hit him hard on the back. No denture. Second bang with the flat of the hand between his shoulder blades – no denture. And it was on number seven that the denture came flying out of his mouth. And I didn't have to do the kiss of life. He breathed like an angry bull for about two minutes. You would've found it very disturbing to see that man breathe. But just as the ambulance arrived, he was breathing and he was beginning to come round. They took him away anyway because he needed to be medically examined for any serious results of his experience. But I think he was going to be alright.

Now that's a good example of where you as first aider have got the casualty's life literally in your hands. You are the difference between life and death. And that's not dramatic – that's fact.

At other times, you can find yourself in a far less urgent situation. There's time to stop and think. There's time to consider what to do. This is where you've got to be so careful as a first aider. You've got to recognise what sort of situation it is and, if it's an emergency, act very very quickly.

Oh sorry! I do apologise! Don't please let me do all the talking. Please – I should have said this at the very beginning – interrupt me at any point you like. Is that alright? I would like you to do that.

UNIT 10 ▶   Narrow escape

▶ Focus on listening 1 (p. 184)

A = Presenter   B = Sam Murphy

A   And now we come to the second part of our series 'Young Explorers' and here's Sam Murphy to introduce it.

B   Hello. Today we're going to talk about how you can survive if you ever get lost or stranded in the wilds. I'm going to tell you how you can make a shelter and how to collect emergency water. But first, I want to talk about survival kits.

A   Are those the kits soldiers and explorers carry – with emergency supplies of food?

B   Yes. You may not plan to go to the jungle or desert but a survival kit could still be useful when you're climbing or walking in the countryside. And you don't need to buy a special kit. You can make one yourself from a few odds and ends. I'll explain what you need now so have a pencil and paper ready. The complete kit fits into a matchbox so it's very light and takes up very little room.

A   Into a matchbox? That sounds unbelievable, Sam!

B   Yes. You'd be surprised what you can get in a matchbox. Why don't you try and see?

A   Alright. I've got one here. What do I put in first?

B   The first thing is a fishing line. You can buy one from an angling shop or use any piece of nylon thread.

A   Does it have to be nylon?

B   Yes. Cotton is too weak and it breaks if you catch anything.

A O.K. I've put that in. And to go with the line I expect you need a fishing hook.

B Right! Again you could buy a special fishing hook but a bent pin or nail will do just as well. And next, a razor blade. Be careful, it's sharp!

A What's that for?

B It's for gutting the fish you catch. It's best to use a blade with only one cutting edge if you can find one. They're much easier to handle.

A A blade with one cutting edge. Right. What's next?

B Number four is a plastic bag. Make sure there are no holes in it, though! You'll need the bag for carrying water – and that's essential for survival. You could also use it to cover wounds and protect them from infection, or even as a fishing trap.

A So, a very useful item. I've folded it as small as it will go so as to get it in.

B Good. The next item for the survival kit is a piece of candle.

A To give light?

B Yes. A candle burns more slowly than matches. You can also use candle wax to make things waterproof and I'll say a bit more about that in a minute. And next …

A A balloon! What on earth can you use a balloon for?

B Well, you can use it in the same way as the plastic bag.

A Oh, for carrying water?

B Yes and to cover wounds. It has the advantage that it will stretch too.

A Isn't there a danger of it stretching too much and bursting?

B Yes, so you must take care because if that happened you could lose valuable water. But even a broken balloon can be useful. You can set light to it and it will help to get your fire going.

A Amazing! Right, I've put that in.

B Next, a needle.

A Is that for sewing?

B Yes, or fishing. But you can also use a needle to make a very simple compass. The instructions are on this week's Fact Sheet and we'll be giving the address for that at the end of the programme. And, now a few matches.

A For lighting a fire?

B Yes. These are the most important part of any survival kit because making a fire is essential and it can take a long time. But before you pack them, you must make them waterproof. You can use the candle for that. Melt a bit of wax and dip the matches in it.

A And that will prevent the matches from getting damp?

B Yes, and you also find that it helps the matches to burn longer. Now, can you fit this piece of chalk in?

A Just. What's it for?

B For writing messages or marking trees so that you can leave a trail.

A Is that everything?

B Nearly. There is one last item but it doesn't need to go into the matchbox. It's a whistle and you can wear it round your neck on a piece of string. It's useful for calling for help because it takes less effort than banging or shouting and it can be heard further away.

▶ Focus on listening 2 (p. 190)

S = Sue   R = Roger

S The other thing I was going to ask you was if you've still got the map of Morocco. From when we went there – it must be eight years ago now …

R Should have. I never throw anything away.

S Because Trevor and John are going to Morocco at Easter and I wanted to show them the route we took.

R What – along the coast?

S Well, no. I was thinking of that awful road we took across country. Do you remember? We'd arrived from Spain in the afternoon, hadn't we? And we'd decided to – instead of just staying the night at the port and setting off early …

R To push on.

S Well, not to push on only, but to drive across half the country! Rabat we were going to. Do you remember?

R Yes.

S And to save time, we thought we'd take that minor road, which looked much more direct.

R Saved miles!

S It was marked yellow on the map, wasn't it – which meant it was suitable for cars.

R Only we didn't realise that it had been an unusually wet spring …

S And that the rivers, which would normally have been dry, would be in full flood.

R The thing I remember is bowling along happily, first day of the holiday, quite unconcerned. So unconcerned that when that – do you remember that man who jumped into the middle of the road and tried to make us stop …

S But wasn't it – there were groups of shepherds coming home, weren't there? And as they went past, they shook – they seemed to be shaking their fists at us. And we thought, 'The natives are unfriendly!' And it was only later that we realised they were trying to warn us about the river ahead.

R Well in my memory there was only one. But when we came over a hill and saw the river actually flowing across the road ahead of us!

S And the point was that we could've gone back then, but it was getting quite late. And the road had been pretty bad, hadn't it? Very muddy. So we decided to give it a try. You drove the car very fast at it, I remember, and we got through safely. And then we thought we'd made the right decision, and done really well.

R And we thought that was it.

S Yes. And then, a few miles on, we met another river, a bit deeper!

R And by the time we'd …

S By the time we'd gone through the first one, to go back would've meant going through it again, which we didn't want to risk.

R And even that the car got through safely.

S But when we came to the third river – I'll never forget it! It looked much worse than the other two – a real torrent!

R But we had no choice by then. We had to try and cross it. The worst moment, I remember, was when the engine cut out. The water must have reached the exhaust pipe and it cut out. And then there we were stuck in the middle of this raging river, with our hearts sinking fast. We opened the door, didn't we? And the water came flooding in.

S I opened the door.

R You opened the door. And I remember seeing all our shoes and maps and things bobbing around in the water. It was terrible!

S And the place itself was an absolute wilderness, wasn't it? In the middle of nowhere! That was one of the reasons why our spirits were so low. I mean we sat in the car, in the middle of this river, looked around, and there was no sign of a village or habitation of any kind, as far as the horizon. And yet, being Morocco, in a few minutes this group of children turned up. They ranged from about two to fourteen, didn't they?

R Yes – and they were very cautious. We even had to call them to help us at first. And then they began by pushing from all sides – three or four at the front and three or four at the back! But when we encouraged them to all push in one direction, it worked, eventually. And when the boat – the boat! – when the car was on the bank, we went through our pockets and gave them various …

S No, we looked through our pockets and we hadn't got a single dirham – is it dirham?

R Dirham.

S Dirham. Because it was our first day and we'd arrived in Ceuta, which is still Spanish, and we hadn't changed any money there.

R But we gave them some Spanish and English coins, which they seemed pleased with. Only then they asked for more, so we actually had to shut the doors and drive away, with them running after us – hoping we wouldn't meet another river!

S Which we didn't, luckily! And then, eventually, we came to the main road. It was such a relief to see all the lights!

R Yes and the car was so wet that we stopped at a service station to empty out the car. Do you remember? We emptied everything out, and in the corner of this hot dusty service station we were scooping out river water all over the forecourt!

S Yes, yes! And then later that night ... in fact it must have been something like three in the morning before we finally got to Rabat. It must have taken a long time to get out of that river!

R Wait a moment and I'll just look for the map. Here it is.

S Oh yes. Let's look. Yes, there's Ceuta, in the north, just opposite Gibraltar at the tip of Spain ... and there's Rabat, on the west coast, down on the left there ...

R Yes, I've got it.

S Now we must have come down to Tetouan ...

R We must have gone through Tetouan.

S Yes. And then ...

R We must have taken that little road to the west, cutting the corner and by-passing Chaoen and Ouezzane.

S Yes, that's where it was – and you can even see the three rivers! Then we must have come to the main road there at Ksar el ... Ksar el Kebir.

R Well be sure to tell Trevor and John to check the weather forecast if they're thinking of following our route!

UNIT 11 ▶ The market place

▶ Focus on listening 1 (p. 200)

I don't suppose there are many people who actually enjoy shopping. I mean the daily or weekly shopping trip for food and the other boring, necessary things of life, like soap powder and toothpaste. Up to now, we've had to do our shopping by going to the shops. And after we've queued in the village store or supermarket, we've got to carry our purchases home.

Well now the microchip has come to our aid! Computers are being used to develop shopping systems which will allow us to do our shopping from home. In fact we'll be able to gather information about products, compare prices and buy goods without even leaving the house!

A scheme especially for pensioners was introduced by Gateshead Council earlier this year. It's called the 'Over 60s Shopping Line' and it allows elderly people to order anything from a bag of chips to chemist's products from their own homes. They use specially adapted televisions, directly linked by telephone to the council's shopping and information service. At the touch of a button, they can order any one of 1,000 items at the town's main supermarket and a range of other items from the local baker and chemist. The goods are delivered to their home within a few hours and this service is completely free.

A similar scheme in Birmingham was started last year through British Telecom, the company which runs the national telephone service. This scheme is called 'Club 403' and it is available to anyone with a telephone who pays extra for British Telecom's special information service. 'Club 403' allows you to use your telephone to contact the local hypermarket's computer. Information is displayed on your television screen and orders can be placed for any of 10,000 goods stored on the computer. The goods are then automatically delivered to your home.

'Club 403' has proved extremely useful to many a busy working person and parent. Members of the club use their telephone and television set to order groceries, frozen food, fresh food and vegetables, bread and meat. They choose what they want, when they

want to have it delivered (day or evening) and the delivery service is free. The only cost to a Club member is £6.50 every three months for the special information service.

For people who live in south London, there's a scheme called 'Shopping Link' which promises all the advantages of a supermarket – such as low costs, variety, freshness and quality, together with a delivery service up to ten o'clock at night. You place your order by telephone but you have to give 24 hours' notice. When the order arrives, you pay £1.73 on top of the bill for the service. You also get a computer printout of your order so you can check off what you've bought.

Finally, there's a scheme called 'Comp-u-card' which is based in Windsor. This system stores information about products in its computer and goods are supplied directly to customers from a nationwide network of manufacturers and distributors. Because no actual stock is held, costs are greatly reduced and 'Comp-u-card' offers the lowest prices in Britain! If a customer can prove that a product he or she has bought is available from somewhere else for less money, 'Comp-u-card' will refund the difference to the customer.

This service costs £20 to join and purchases can be made by cheque or credit card.

▶ Focus on listening 2 (p. 202)

I = Interviewer   A = Auctioneer

I Well, it's ... it's very interesting to meet you, Mr Ewing. I've often wanted to talk to an auctioneer and I wonder, can you tell me how you actually became an auctioneer?

A Purely by accident, like most things in life ... um ... I joined a firm of chartered surveyors when I came out of Polytechnic, having qualified in fact as a property surveyor, and they happened to have an auction room as part of their business. And I became very interested in that, which really revived an interest that I'd had with my family when I was younger, and an opportunity came up to move into the auction side of the business which I took very gratefully, and haven't looked back since.

I Can I ask you about what people do when they want to make a bid, when they want to offer some money? What's the most usual thing that they do to show you that?

A Well, the auction obviously is described in a catalogue which is normally just a very rough-printed paper, um, description, and that is often the instrument that they use to actually accept the bid which the auctioneer offers. The auctioneer basically starts the bidding, asks for a bid from the room, offers the lot and if a person in the room wishes to accept that offer they either raise a hand or, if they obviously have a pre-arranged signal which is what often people think happens most of the time, they wink or touch their nose or scratch their head. But normally it's raising the catalogue or raising an arm just to say 'I accept that offer.'

I And I have to ask you, has it ever happened that somebody really was scratching their head and not making a bid?

A Yes, it ... it does happen but it's often a bit of a joke and the auctioneer knows very well that they're just waving to someone on the other side of the room and, for a bit of light relief, it's nice just to sort of make the point that you should definitely raise your catalogue if you actually wish to accept the bid.

I So you give somebody a shock but it's not ... they don't have to go away with the goods afterwards?

A I think it's very important and an auctioneer will always try and keep a little bit of entertainment going, because after all it can get terribly dull if you're just there and things are being sold and nothing else is happening. And one of the joys of an auction is that anything can happen, um, you get people getting what they call 'auction fever', which is basically getting slightly carried away, shall we say. You get a lot of excitement and one of the skills of an auctioneer is to control the room and to encourage that sort of relaxed but competitive atmosphere, and it's gimmicks like, um, asking the lady whether she was in fact bidding £500 when she's just come into the room to wave hello to her mother on the other side that makes it a little bit more interesting.

I   Has there been a really memorable sale in your mind, or an item which reached a really surprising price?

A   Yes, oh, very many. Um, I suppose as far as sales are concerned, one of the ... always the more interesting sales tend to be where you're selling up the contents of a large house when the family have moved or decided to move, specifically the sort of country house type. And they're the sales that always seem to encourage a lot of people to want to go and have a look around the house as well as the contents. They're always very well, er,

I   ... attended.

A   ... attended. And you can get some very big surprises in those sort of sales. I remember a painting which in fact we discovered in the coal hole of a very large house, just south of Bristol, which was in an appalling condition – you could hardly see what was actually underneath it – and we ended up by selling it for £3,500 ... um ... and that was really, we were hoping that it would get something around there, but it was a very speculative thing and it was nice to actually have got a very good price for it, which I think it was a very good price for it.

I   Yes ...

A   In the same auction, in fact, we had a very large bedroom suite, which we sold for £25,000, and again part of the suite was a four-poster bed and we found part of the four-poster bed in one of the outhouses, we found the uprights in the swimming pool and we found the rest of the bed literally scattered around in cupboards all round the house.

I   Have you found that you've become very interested in a particular area of, well, antiques or collectibles or whatever, yourself?

A   Um, yes, I mean, it's difficult because being what we call a provincial auctioneer, in other words, not being in a very large organisation I'm called upon to value items in a very broad sense. In other words, I have to do jewellery as well as rugs, pictures, furniture, right the way through, anything that you'd find in somebody's house, so I have to make sure that my interest, shall we say, is generalist. My personal taste, I suppose, tends to follow that interest. I wouldn't be doing what I'm doing after all if I'm doing it well, unless I was interested in it, and I suppose my ... I prefer ... I like furniture, I like wood, I like the feel of wood and I like the look of wood and I very much admire the craftsmanship that you get in wood. That is probably my preference. One of the problems of being an auctioneer is that you tend to see items which you would like to own but you can't afford. And because you see the nice items, you don't really want to own the items which you can afford so you're in a bit of a cleft stick, but that's life.

I   One last question ... if you had to give advice to somebody who had never been to an auction but wanted to, what would you say?

A   Don't be scared and do it. It's much easier to bid at an auction than you think and I think it's exciting. If you're bored by walking round a supermarket or going to a shop, go to an auction and I think it will change your attitude on the way that items can be bought and sold. Go and try it.

I   Fine. Thank you very much.

UNIT 12 ▶ Turning points

▶ **Focus on listening 1 (p. 215)**

A = Presenter   B = Brian Collins   C = William Rudd
D = Patricia Pole   E = Graham Clarke

A   Unfortunately redundancy is a fact of life in Britain these days. And whether you work for a big multi-national company, or a small family firm, it can happen to anyone. Thousands of people have lost their jobs through redundancy in recent years. But with each lost job, there is the so-called 'golden handshake'. What do people do with this money? Do they spend it all on luxuries? Invest it? Or use it to start their own small business? We report on four cases of people who used their redundancy money to change their lives.

Brian Collins is 34. Until he was in his late twenties, he had a well-paid, responsible job in the electrical industry. But he suddenly realised that he could be worried to death by the time he was 30. Then, when he was offered a job in Scotland teaching sailing, he decided to take the opportunity to do something completely different. Four years later, however, the firm he was working for got into difficulties and Brian was made redundant.

B   I spent the £350 I received in redundancy money on a holiday in Tenerife! And while I was there, I lay on the beach in the sun wondering what on earth I was going to do. In the end, I decided to go back to Scotland and start my own boat repair firm.

A   Brian didn't expect to make much money from boat repairs, and at first he needed the £40 a week he received in a government grant. Now, eight months later, his income is £20,000 – much more than he would be earning in industry. And he enjoys working for himself.

B   Yes, I'm much happier than I was when I was working for someone else, and I've had fewer sleepless nights this year than I did last year when I was worried about whether I might upset the boss!

A   William Rudd is 54 now. He worked for a multi-national chemical company for 20 years until 1980 when he decided to take early retirement. He says he'd known for about a year that he was going to leave and he'd been applying for office jobs. When he didn't get anywhere, he decided to use his redundancy money of £70,000 to open a butcher's shop in central London. He started in July – the worst time for a butcher's shop like his, unfortunately, and his overdraft just kept going up.

C   I managed to spend far too much money on doing the place up because I didn't want it to look too ordinary. It was all rather frightening because there was nobody between me and the bank manager! I don't know if what I did was brave or foolish – a bit of both, I suppose.

A   But at the same time, William was enjoying himself. It was fun serving behind the counter in the shop – completely different from his previous job, and much harder work. And his business is going from strength to strength. In fact, he has just opened a second London shop.

A   Patricia and Rex Pole are a married couple who both worked for a bank until they were made redundant three years ago. With their redundancy money they bought a public house on the south coast of England.

D   The terms of the redundancy payment were based on the number of years you had worked in the bank. Between us we had done 33 years, so it was quite a good sum. It gave us approximately £30,000.

A   In fact, a couple of years earlier, they had started thinking about going into the pub business. When they found a place they wanted to buy, they put all their redundancy money into it.

D   If we'd known what it would be like, I don't think we would have done it. It was absolutely awful to start with. We didn't know anything about running a pub – although we thought we did! We'd never had to worry about paying bills before. And we ran the pub totally by ourselves which meant a seven-day week and terribly long hours. It was very physical work too, you're on your feet all the time and the first two months were very very hard. We hardly spoke to each other. Actually we were in a state of shock!

A   After 14 months, they decided to sell.

D   We realised we couldn't imagine spending the rest of our lives doing that kind of work. We wanted to have a private life again!

A   Patricia and Rex Pole have now returned to work in banking but they're glad to have tried the experiment.

A   Finally, we have Graham Clarke who is 57. He worked for 27 years as a salesman in Colchester.

E   I actually asked to be made redundant because I could see that things weren't going very well for the company. My rounds were getting smaller and smaller, and more branches were closing down.

A   He was made redundant in February and received £2,000 in redundancy pay.

E   I started working on the idea of becoming a magician because magic has been my hobby for nearly 40 years. I thought, 'I've got a good collection of tricks, so I might as well see if I can make a living out of magic.'

A   He started his business in July under the name of Graham Clarke Magic, and the first step was to contact agents and to advertise in the local newspaper. He was also interviewed on local radio.

E   I don't expect to make any money for at least a year because you need to spend at least a third of your income on advertising. I'll know how I stand by next January and then, if things are going well, it'll still take another year to eighteen months to start to establish the business properly.

A   Graham has already worked at a number of children's parties and he plans to do after-dinner acts as well. He is hoping to be able to work all over the country and even abroad and we wish him, and everyone else who has proved there can be life after redundancy, well.

▶ Focus on listening 2 (p. 222)

A = Interviewer   B = John

A   John, when we talked last time you told me about your long career in the Merchant Navy. That lasted for ...?

B   It lasted for ... 12 years, in all.

A   And you said it was your friends who finally persuaded you to make the break and leave.

B   Yes.

A   Well, after that I know you started a completely new career in a hospital, working as a male nurse. Tell me how that came about.

B   I was in hospital for about six weeks, and while I was there I was thinking what to do. I absolutely didn't want to go back in the Merchant Navy. I'd actually got to the end of that then! I don't think that while I was in hospital I actually considered

nursing as a possibility, but when I came out – it was very awkward. Because when I left the Merchant Navy I was 31, and pretty well untrained for anything, really. I mean, I could wait at table and mix cocktails and make crepes suzettes, and things – so I could have worked in a hotel, I suppose. But that would have been like leaving the Merchant Navy and starting to do more or less the same thing as what I'd been doing. But it would've been worse because the pay wouldn't have been so good. And there's not many things that you can actually train for when you're 31 ... And ... um ... God bless nursing because they'll take people up to the age of 50 provided they have the right educational qualifications. And it all suddenly became very attractive. I remembered seeing the nurses work in hospital, and I thought, 'I'd quite like to do that' and I had the right qualifications and they were very short of nurses at that time.

A   Where did you start?

B   I started where I finished – at Frenchay Hospital in Bristol. I went for an interview there and I knew immediately that it was a nice place to work. And I never left it.

A   So they accepted you?

B   They accepted me, believe it or not!

A   How long was the training?

B   Three years, initially. I did three years general nurse training, and then I did two years training in mental illness. And it was marvellous!

A   Were you trained as a male nurse, or just as ... a nurse?

B   There is really no difference. When I started, there were seven other men in the group I was in. Now, compared with today, that's very high. Because today you might get one man in a class of twenty. So there were a lot coming into the profession then.

A   What were the hours then?

B   Forty hours a week.

A   Is that the same now?

B   It's $37\frac{1}{2}$ now.

A   And how did the pay compare with being in the Merchant Navy?

B   The pay was very low compared with the Merchant Navy. It was very difficult to live on. During the three years that I ... that I did nurse training, I spent almost all my own savings.

A   Were most people who did that training in their teens?

B   Oh yes.

A   And were they living at home?

B   Some were. Some were living in the nurses' home. The nurses' pay was reasonable if you lived in the nurses' home and ate at the hospital. But obviously, as a 31 year old, I didn't want to be living in the nurses' home. And when I found – even though it was a very small place to live – it was impossible not to dip into savings.

A   And did you ever question whether you were doing the right thing?

B   Oh no, never! It was the most marvellous time. In fact the training was the best part of the nursing. I've never enjoyed any of it as much as I enjoyed the three years' training.

A   Why was that?

B   Well, when you're a student, for one thing, you're having new experiences all the time. So that, once you've trained, and you take on a post in a ward, it becomes very routine. When you're a student, you do two months on an orthopaedic ward, and then you go for a month on a children's ward, then you go into the operating theatre for two months. So there's constant change. And it was a bit like being in the Merchant Navy because ...

instead of travelling from country to country, I was moving
from ward to ward!

A   So how did you go from that into nurse teaching?

B   I think I got into teaching because I wanted to go on learning,
while I was on the ward, so I did other courses as well as the
basic training. And it was the next logical step. I remember my
tutor saying 'Well, now you've got the Diploma of Nursing, and
you've done all that you can do, have you ever thought about
teaching?' Because they've always been very short of nurse
teachers. They're always looking for nurse teachers.

A   Is that because there aren't many people who can teach?

B   Oh, I don't think being able to teach has got much to do with
being a nurse teacher! It's very easy to say why they've always
been short of nurse teachers. Because nurse teachers are paid
exactly the same as ordinary nurses and you have to do all the
extra work yourself without any extra pay. Anyway, I went
away for a year and did a Certificate of Education.

A   And was it worthwhile?

B   Oh yes! I really enjoyed it. It was very very good to be away
and to spend all your spare time studying.

A   Do you regret at all that you didn't start nursing much earlier?

B   No. I have no regrets in my life whatsoever. Even the bad things
I don't regret. And I certainly don't regret spending my
formative years going round the world. I don't think that I
could ever have had anything to equal that, had I stayed on at
school. Because I virtually went everywhere and saw an awful
lot, and I don't think I'd have got that any other way. If I'd gone
straight into nursing, I'd probably have got bored with it by
now.

EXAM PRACTICE: Tapescripts

▶ SITUATIONS 1 (p. 255)

One

Man	Oh no, I don't believe it.
Woman	What? What are you talking about?
Man	Just look. The side window. It's been smashed.
Woman	Your briefcase. You didn't leave it on the back seat, did you?
Man	No, I'm not that stupid. I put it in the boot.
Woman	You'd better see if it's still there.
Man	OK, OK. Let's get the boot open ... Yes, there it is. Thank goodness for that!
Woman	Could have been worse then. What do we do now?
Man	We'd better go and report it, and then see about getting this window fixed, I suppose.

Two

I'm sorry, I don't know the title. All I can remember is that it's got
the name of a flower in it. And there was a film based on it, with
Dolly Parton in, I think, but I don't know what that was called
either. And I can't remember the author but I'd know the name if I
heard it. It's just come out as a paperback – I read a review of it in
the paper last week. You must know the one I mean. I'd like to buy a
copy as a birthday present for my mother.

Three

Good afternoon. Well, first if I can just reassure listeners there was
no danger to any of the passengers. As you say, the aircraft took off
in stormy conditions and was actually struck shortly after take-off.
That's not unusual. It doesn't happen every day but it's not unusual
and of course aircraft do have equipment to protect them from
lightning. But the captain reported that it was a particularly loud
bang and he decided to land so that our engineers could check the
aircraft.

Four

Woman 1	Have you got your ticket?
Woman 2	Yes, I think it's here somewhere. Is this it?
Woman 1	That's it. I'm not sure if it'll be ready yet, but I'll have a look. What was it?
Woman 2	A man's grey suit.
Woman 1	You may be in luck. Just a minute. (*brief pause*) Yes, here we are.
Woman 2	Oh, good. Could I just check it? There was a mark on the lapel. Let's see ... Yes, you've done a lovely job. Great. How much is that?

Five

Can you turn round? No don't look at me, I don't want you to pose.
Look away, if you can. That's it. Hold it. Oh no, someone's in the
way – would you mind? Thank you *very* much! Just a sec. The sun's
going in. No it's OK, I think. Here goes then – try not to blink. That's
it. Hope it comes out now.

Six

Hi, it's me. I'm really sorry ... Yes, I do know how important the
meeting is ... No, no, I wouldn't let you down, you know me. I've
just been a bit held up, that's all. Not my fault. We've had these
inspectors in all day – it's been a bit of a nightmare, to be honest. I
didn't even get any lunch ... OK, OK calm down. I'll grab something
to eat on my way over there.

Seven

A   I just can't get it to work.

B   Have you switched it on?

A   Eh?

B   Take the earphones off a minute. I said "Have you switched it on?"

A   Yes, of course I have, but nothing's happening.

B   Are you sure it's plugged in?

A   I didn't check. Is it?

B   Yes. Let me see – oh, I see what's wrong. You've got it on 'Pause'. There. Can you hear anything now?

A   Yes, very faintly. How do you turn it up? Oh that's it. Great.

Eight

You're going to be in all morning, aren't you? I was just wondering if you could do me a favour. You know that set of mugs I sent off for ages ago, for Julia's birthday? Well, anyway I rang the company up about it and they said it should arrive some time this morning. The thing is I've got to go out and someone'll need to sign for it. Could you do that? I'd be really grateful …

▶ WILDLIFE ARTIST (p. 256)

Interviewer: Today I'm talking to Kevin Simpson, who is one of our most successful wildlife artists. Kevin, welcome. Tell me, when did you first start drawing?

Kevin Simpson: Oh, I've been drawing for as long as I can remember. I first started by copying pictures out of magazines and I suppose I was probably about 6 or 7 then. I've always loved animals. But it wasn't until I was about 20, I guess, that I really developed my own style and the pictures began to sell.

Interviewer: How do you go about drawing an animal?

Kevin Simpson: I start by taking photographs and then I work from the photo to do the drawing. It's not the way most artists like to work, actually, but it's the way I prefer. With a photograph you can take as much time as you like getting the details right, you see, whereas with a live animal it's more difficult, obviously. And that's what I really enjoy – the detailed work, even though it does take quite a bit of time. It's one of the things people seem to like about my pictures as well – the detailed work.

Interviewer : One of the more unusual animals you've drawn is the wolf, isn't it? How did that come about? I mean wolves wouldn't be everyone's first choice of subject and I shouldn't imagine they 're that easy to find, are they?

Kevin Simpson: Well, not in the wild, no, they're pretty rare nowadays. But I did my drawings at a wonderful wolf sanctuary they have in Portugal. I was invited there by the wildlife charity that runs it and I spent a couple of weeks photographing them and getting to know them generally.

Interviewer: And did you learn to love them?

Kevin Simpson: Yes I did, actually. I was able to go into the wolves' enclosures and spend time with them, and little by little I got them to trust me. They even used to lick my hands, you know. And it's quite something putting your fingers into a wolf's mouth, I can tell you! They have the most massive jaws. It was an amazing experience.

Interviewer: What sort of materials do you use? Do you paint as well as draw, for example?

Kevin Simpson: No, I stick to drawing. And I just use pencils, that's all I need. I use everything from the hardest available down to the softest 3B. And sometimes I also rub the pencil lines with tissue paper afterwards to give a softer, smoother effect.

Interviewer: Did you have pets as a child?

Kevin Simpson: Yes, we always had animals around when I was young – not the usual, you know, cats and dogs, but there was a rabbit, for example, and there was also a goat called Basil – lovely old chap he was. We had a pet fox at one time too, I remember. He'd been abandoned by his mother and eventually he went back to the wild. But I wasn't very good at looking after the animals, I'm afraid. That was my brother's job!

Interviewer: What do you think about keeping animals in captivity?

Kevin Simpson: I can't say I really like zoos. I know they're supposed to be educational and all that but what makes me sad is that the animals have no purpose, no purpose at all. I mean they don't have to find food for themselves and they don't have to worry about being eaten. So they're just there to be looked at. And that doesn't seem right to me.

▶ TRANSPORT (p. 256)

1

It's stupid really because I have to leave so early to avoid the traffic that I'm in the office nearly an hour before everyone else, once I've found a meter, of course, which is easier said than done. And the costs mount up – fuel, repairs and all that. But I can't face the alternative: rushing for the 7.45 every morning, standing all the way. No, I like my little bit of independence, you know: cruising along, music on nice and loud.

2

There are lots of advantages. It's great in traffic jams because you can sail right up to the front of the queue and it also keeps you fit, obviously. But the best thing is that it doesn't cost you a penny in fuel. The main disadvantage is that you seem to be invisible to a lot of drivers. They just don't see you. Or they open their door just as you're coming by, that's another one! I've had a couple of near misses that way.

3

I don't mind the journey. It gives me a chance to read the papers, think a bit. I'm lucky because I get on near the beginning of the route so I generally get a seat. It can't be much fun if you have to stand. But the journey takes longer these days now they've done away with conductors and the driver has to sell the tickets.

4

I don't enjoy it much. I know it sounds glamorous but to me it's just a necessary evil. There's all that waiting around before you get on board. And then the seats just aren't designed for people like me with long legs so I tend to end up with cramp. I generally try to get a bit of sleep but they will keep waking you up to serve the meals. And the food! I won't go on …

5

There's nothing like it as far as I'm concerned. You can keep your fast cars. I just love being out there on the ocean, all on my own, with nothing but the sound of wind in the sails. It's incredibly relaxing. I try not to use the engine unless I absolutely have to. It's pretty noisy and it's not that reliable anyway. Hey, why not come out with me some time?

BUDDY DOGS (p. 256)

Reporter: According to experts, stroking an animal can lower your blood pressure and give you a feeling of calm. Well that's great news if you've got a pet, but what if you can't get hold of one? That's where organisations like Buddy Dogs come in. They take dogs to people who can't have animals of their own because they're living in hospitals and residential homes. Linda Donoghue met up with a black labrador called Dan and his owner, Andrew, to see what's in a day's work for a Buddy Dog.

Andrew: He was going to training school and he had such a fantastic nature, so when I read about the Buddy Dog scheme it just occurred to me what a wonderful thing it would be if he could use his training to bring joy to people in their retirement. That's how it started.

Linda Donoghue: How old is Dan? And how long has he been a Buddy Dog?

Andrew: He's four years old now though people think he's older than that because he's so sensible. I had him when he was about three months old. Having seen him I knew there was something special about that dog. And my instinct proved absolutely right. I'm one of those people that believe if you want a dog, don't go looking for a dog, you must let the dog find you. And he found me and he proved absolutely brilliant. Anyway, we started with the scheme about eighteen months ago, I suppose it must be now.

L D: So he obviously really enjoys visiting the elderly people then.

Andrew: Oh, he absolutely loves it. Yes, it's his life almost. And he just loves anyone that will make a fuss of him, whether it's children or anything. He's just got such a lovely nature and he's absolutely 100% trustworthy. It's, it's so good for the old folk to be able to stroke an animal and be close. Especially when they've had pets all their life and then find themselves having to come into a home and not being able to bring their pets with them. It must be very, very sad for them.

L D: Now Dan's obviously very well behaved. If someone wanted to get involved with the scheme, would their dog have to go through special training?

Andrew: Well, it certainly helps but I don't think it's absolutely necessary. I wouldn't say it needs to be a super dog but it certainly needs to be a dog with a calm, gentle nature. And I had to answer lots of questions before he was accepted.

L D: Now they've got a cat here as well. How does Dan get on with the cat?

Andrew: He's used to cats. In fact, I've got a neighbour whose cat absolutely hates dogs but because Dan is so still and gentle their cat doesn't mind him at all. I've never ever seen him chase cats. He's used to horses too and all sorts of animals. I think that's quite important because coming to a home like this, they can meet other animals and the last thing you want is a dog that's going to turn nasty.

L D: What kind of initial reaction did you get when you first brought Dan here?

Andrew: Oh, the people here were absolutely thrilled to see him and now I can't come here enough. Their eyes light up as soon as he comes through the door. The biggest problem I find with this job is that they all want to spoil him. And I have to try and stop them giving him too many little bits, biscuits and things, 'cos he's a greedy dog. Aren't you?

L D: Are there any other places that you think Buddy Dogs could be useful?

Andrew: Yes, I'd like to see them used as much as possible in prisons. With young offenders. I think that the unconditional love that the dog gives would be absolutely wonderful for some of these people that experience very little love in their lives.

Reporter: That's Linda Donoghue finding out all about the Buddy Dog scheme.

SITUATIONS 2 (p. 257)

One

Hi, it's me, Sally. Look I don't know if you remembered but it's Malcolm's birthday next Thursday and I thought we ought to celebrate somehow. I hope you're free 'cos I was thinking of doing something special for supper. He's always going on about haggis – being a Scotsman! – and I thought I'd have a go at making some, and also some treacle pudding, his favourite. Would you be able to give me a hand preparing them?

Two

Man	I'm pretty sure it was on this level.
Woman	You mean you didn't make a note of the level?
Man	No, but we were in a hurry. I thought I'd recognise it.
Woman	This doesn't look familiar at all.
Man	No, it doesn't. Let's go down a level.
Woman	We could be here all day at this rate!
Man	Now don't start!
Woman	Isn't that it over there? See? In the corner.
Man	Except we parked in the middle of a row, remember? We'll just have to start at the top and work down.
Woman	Great!

Three

I went to the ski school they had but I wasn't that keen on the instructor. He was only about 18 but he was like some sort of sergeant major in the army. Every time somebody fell over, he'd shout at them: 'You ... follow me!' And you knew you were in trouble. I did make some progress in the end but you had to keep reminding yourself that you were on holiday and that it was supposed to be fun.

Four

Oh, come on. It's only for the weekend. Two days! You'll hardly miss it. And you wouldn't be using it anyway. It's not much to ask – I'd do the same for you any time. And you needn't worry, I won't damage it or anything. Ask Julia – she'll tell you what a careful driver I am. It'll make all the difference to have a car. OK? Just this once?

Five

There are delays on the B748 between Heathfield and Brayside as a result of an overturned tanker, and you are advised to avoid the area if you can. Elsewhere, there are temporary traffic lights in operation on the Leighton by-pass. Delays in both directions, I'm afraid. No reports of any problems on the Avon Bridge so far this evening. That's all for now.

Six

Hello. Can you put me through to the Customer Services Department please?
(brief pause)
Hello. Yes, I hope so. I bought one of your washing machines a month ago and ...
(brief pause)
You're the Marketing Department? I'm sorry, I don't know how that happened. Can you put me back to the switchboard?
(brief pause)
Hello, I asked to speak to the Customer Services Department but I got ...
(brief pause)
Hello, hello ... oh no I've been cut off. This is hopeless!

Seven

Customer	They're just a bit too long, don't you think? Is there any chance they could be shortened?
Assistant	It's easy to do, you know, you could do it yourself.
Customer	No, I'm hopeless at sewing, I'm afraid.

Assistant	If you can pop back this afternoon, I could probably do them for you then. There'd be a small charge, I'm afraid.
Customer	That's fine.
Assistant	How much do you want off? Can you show me?
Customer	About a centimetre, I should think. So they're just above the floor at the back – like that.

Eight

At that point, I was a housewife with no work, no income and my children were leaving home. Then I saw an advert in the paper for a part-time degree course in art and design, and I thought 'Great. This is just what I need. It'll do wonders for my self-confidence and I know I can do it. I know I'm not stupid. So it'll help me get back to normal. And it'll give me so much work that I won't have time to think about what's happened.'

► EXTRAS (p. 258)

Presenter

I wonder if you've ever fancied appearing in a film. Because, if so, here's your chance. There are parts going in a film that's being made in a couple of weeks time right here in this city. They're looking for men and women of all ages, and Caroline Bailey, who's the film's assistant director, has joined me in the studio. Good morning Caroline. (*Good morning*) First of all, tell us a little bit about the film.

Caroline

It's about a young girl who's a talented pianist. And the film's about an accident that happens and how it affects her life and her relationship with her boyfriend, Nick. But it's not all tragic, it's also very funny in places. And it's very romantic at times, too.

Presenter

Now you're here to find extras, aren't you? Between 300 and 550 you want, is that right?

Caroline

That's about right – we can't be more precise than that at the moment. There are all kind of parts for all kinds of people. For some special parts we're looking for particular types of people, I have to say. For example, we need a really tall gentleman, to appear in one scene – a fight scene. So there are some interesting parts and then there's more ordinary background action of just being, you know, part of a crowd.

Presenter

And if you're looking for someone to play a specific part like the very tall gentleman you just mentioned, do they need to have basic acting skills or can anyone do it?

Caroline

Yes. For that sort of part we would want people with some acting skills. If people are used to appearing on the stage, they're not going to be shy about acting in front of a camera. Because if people are nervous or shy, a lot of time can get wasted. And also we like to use people who have an interest in film and television – they tend to make better extras because they enjoy the chance to see the film industry at work and to see exactly how a film is made.

Presenter

Right. So what does being an extra involve? First of all, what's the pay like?

Caroline

It's not bad. I mean people should come away with at least thirty pounds a day even if they just appear in a crowd scene. Not that it's only about money, but we feel people should get a decent amount for their work. And you're also fed, you know. Oh yes, you get two meals a day as well. We do try to look after people!

Presenter

OK. So what kind of things are you asking people to do?

Caroline

Not a lot. For most of the parts we just need people with the right look. Each scene is set in a different location with a different crowd. One scene is in a hotel, so we need businessmen and receptionists for that, then there's a scene in a disco where I'm going to need a young crowd. Most people I would say should be in their mid-twenties to early thirties because our actors are in that age group. But we do need some older people too.

Presenter

And how long are you going to be filming for?

Caroline

Four weeks. From Monday week, which is what? The thirteenth.

Presenter

So anyone listening now who wants to be a film extra, what do they do? Where do they meet you?

Caroline

They should come to the Arts Club in Redland Street on Tuesday evening. We'll meet anybody that turns up. We'll take your details, check when you're available, and so on.

Presenter

So there you are, it's next Tuesday evening at the Arts Club if you want to take part in this film. Caroline, thanks for being with us this afternoon.

► MEMORIES (p. 259)

1

What happened was, on a Monday we were given an hour to write an essay. And that night he would take the books home with him. The next day, when we came in in the morning, all the books were laid out on the desks. Now, if you had three mistakes such as you'd left out a comma or you hadn't used a capital letter, you were punished, with a cane, whack. One particular day, he went round and caned every single kid in the form. (*laughs*)

2

Oh, it was different before the war. There were some very large stores and outside they had glass showcases with all the goods in, you know. There was always a man on the door, a real gentleman, who asked you which department you wanted, then took you up to a counter and and put a chair for you to sit on. Yes, you never had to stand up. I found the assistants much politer then than they are today.

3

I only remember going away once in the whole of my childhood, and that was for a week in Weston. We stayed in rooms in a house - not in a hotel or anything. Usually my mother bought the food and the landlady cooked it for us. And there were so many things for us children to do – fishing for crabs; we used to play on the rocks near the pier, collect shells, all those sorts of things. It was wonderful.

4

I've been to the Bristol City ground when there were 20,000 supporters and I suppose the total number of police was only about a dozen, and most of those were on traffic duty outside. Once or twice there might have been a bit of an argument because one bloke followed City and the other was a Rovers supporter but then all that happened was that a policeman would come over and say "Come on chaps, act your age." and that would be the end of it.

5

There were no modern conveniences in those days. There was a larder, quite a big larder, with a marble slab to put your butter on. And a cover for the meat to keep the flies off. And you also had a boiler that you put on the stove. It was a tiny gas stove, all black. And you put the boiler on the stove and boiled up all the washing in it, which took ages because it was so small. But they're quite good memories really.

▶ COMPETITION (P. 259)

Presenter
Well, I hope I've come to the right place. I'm at the York House Restaurant, which is a really beautiful country house I have to tell you, and I'm hoping to meet two young people who've qualified for the final of the Young Waiter or Waitress of the Year Competition. Let's go inside and meet them ... I think this is the room. Yes. Hello, you must be Colin and Jennie? Good, I am in the right place! Let's talk first of all to Colin. Colin, now you and Jennie have reached the final of the competition – and there are, how many is it? Twelve finallists? [**Colin**: *That's right*] Twelve finallists, so you've done fantastically well. Tell me all about the competition and then we'll find out about how you and Jennie are going to approach the final.

Colin
Yes, certainly. The competition is to find the young waiter or waitress of the year, and it's a national competition. It starts with regional heats in the major cities around the country and Jennie and I have been lucky enough to win through the regional heats and we now go to the national final which will be held at the Savoy Hotel in London .

Presenter
OK. And I understand you were up against three hundred and fifty other entrants at the start. So you've had to beat all those other people in order to get through to the finals – that's a lot.

Colin
That's right. It's quite a lot but the competition is in its fifth year now and it's become very popular.

Presenter
Let's have a word now with Jennie. Why do you think there's such an interest in the competition?

Jennie
Well, if you do well it's obviously very good for your career, you can put it on your CV. And it's good publicity for the restaurant you work for as well. My boss was very keen for me to enter ... And if you actually win, you get a holiday in New York with visits to the famous restaurants there.

Presenter
So what have you had to do to get this far?

Jennie
There was a written competition and then there were four practical tasks which we had to carry out. We don't know what will happen in the final – you don't get any warning except that we know we'll have to serve lunch to a group of celebrity guests, various famous people, you know.

Presenter
Yes, so they'll get together a group of people who know a lot about food and wine and they'll be playing the part of guests and watching you critically. Can you do any homework for this sort of thing, Colin? I mean obviously you're serving food all the time so you're continually developing your knowledge and experience.

Colin
Yes, hopefully we'll be able to put into practice the training we've had and the skills we use every day, just continue. But there are areas it's useful to study beforehand. With wine, for example, if somebody doesn't like the wine that's served, we'd be expected to suggest a suitable alternative. So you have to know the different characteristics of wine and what goes well with what dishes and so on.

Presenter
I see. Right. Well that was Colin Scott and Jennie Pullen who are in the final of the Young Waiter or Young Waitress of the Year Competition. It's going to be on Monday 23rd of April and we wish you both the very best of luck on the day!

Colin/Jennie
Thanks.

Presenter
And if either of you wins, which we hope you do of course, you'll have to come back and tell us about it.